KOREAN Q&A SENTENCE PATTERNS

—

WRITTEN BY TALK TO ME IN KOREAN

KOREAN Q&A SENTENCE PATTERNS

초판발행	1st edition published	2016. 9. 1
지은이	Written by	TalkToMeInKorean
책임편집	Edited by	선경화 Kyung-hwa Sun, 스테파니 베이츠 Stephanie Bates
디자인	Design by	선윤아 Yoona Sun
삽화	Illustration by	장성원 Sungwon Jang, 선윤아 Yoona Sun
녹음	Voice Recording by	TalkToMeInKorean
펴낸곳	Published by	롱테일북스 Longtail Books
펴낸이	Publisher	이수영 Su Young Lee
편집	Copy-edited by	김보경 Florence Kim
주소	Address	서울 마포구 양화로 12길 16-9(서교동) 북앤드빌딩 3층
		3rd Floor Book-And Bldg. 16-9 Yanghwa-ro 12-gil, Mapo-gu, Seoul, KOREA
전화	Telephone	+82-2-3144-2708
팩스	Fax	+82-2-3144-2597
이메일	E-mail	TTMIK@longtailbooks.co.kr
ISBN	979-11-86701-53-9	13710

KOREAN
Q&A SENTENCE
PATTERNS

한국어 질문 패턴 모음집

• **Category**: There are ten categories in total.

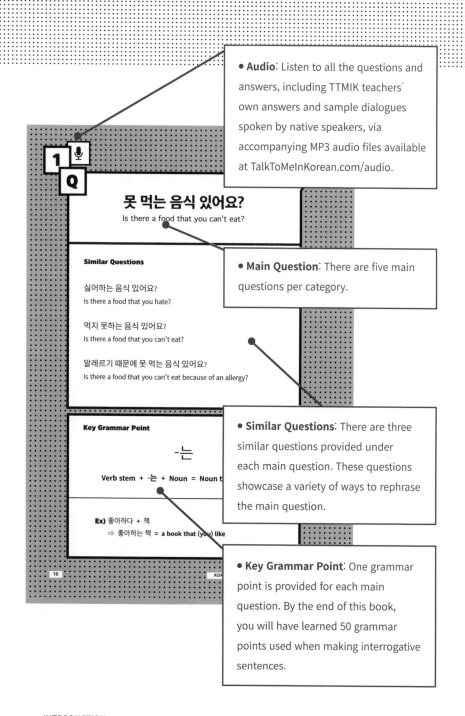

● Audio: Listen to all the questions and answers, including TTMIK teachers' own answers and sample dialogues spoken by native speakers, via accompanying MP3 audio files available at TalkToMeInKorean.com/audio.

1
Q

못 먹는 음식 있어요?
Is there a food that you can't eat?

● Main Question: There are five main questions per category.

Similar Questions

싫어하는 음식 있어요?
Is there a food that you hate?

먹지 못하는 음식 있어요?
Is there a food that you can't eat?

알레르기 때문에 못 먹는 음식 있어요?
Is there a food that you can't eat because of an allergy?

● Similar Questions: There are three similar questions provided under each main question. These questions showcase a variety of ways to rephrase the main question.

Key Grammar Point

-는

Verb stem + -는 + Noun = Noun t

Ex) 좋아하다 + 책
⇨ 좋아하는 책 = a book that (you) like

● Key Grammar Point: One grammar point is provided for each main question. By the end of this book, you will have learned 50 grammar points used when making interrogative sentences.

16   KOR

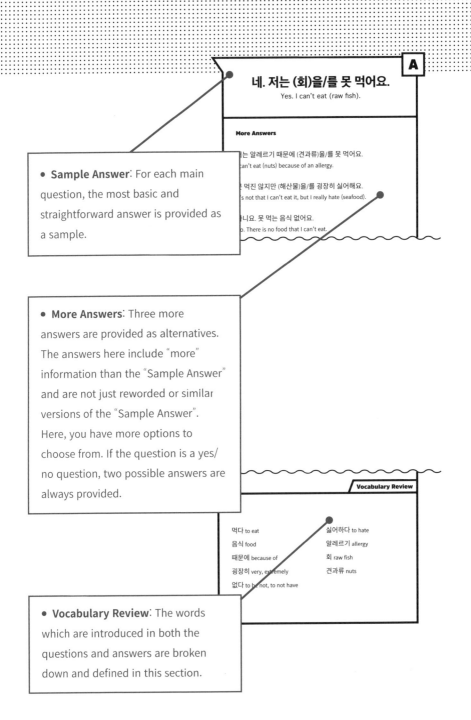

A

네. 저는 (회)을/를 못 먹어요.
Yes. I can't eat (raw fish).

More Answers

는 알레르기 때문에 (견과류)을/를 못 먹어요.
can't eat (nuts) because of an allergy.

먹진 않지만 (해산물)을/를 굉장히 싫어해요.
's not that I can't eat it, but I really hate (seafood).

니요. 못 먹는 음식 없어요.
o. There is no food that I can't eat.

- **Sample Answer**: For each main question, the most basic and straightforward answer is provided as a sample.

- **More Answers**: Three more answers are provided as alternatives. The answers here include "more" information than the "Sample Answer" and are not just reworded or similar versions of the "Sample Answer". Here, you have more options to choose from. If the question is a yes/no question, two possible answers are always provided.

Vocabulary Review

먹다 to eat
음식 food
때문에 because of
굉장히 very, extremely
없다 to be not, to not have

싫어하다 to hate
알레르기 allergy
회 raw fish
견과류 nuts

- **Vocabulary Review**: The words which are introduced in both the questions and answers are broken down and defined in this section.

못 먹는 음식 있어요?

Kyung-hwa's Answer

저는 회나 육회처럼 익히지 않은 음식은 못 먹어요. 억지로라도 먹어 보려고 시도해 본 적이 있는데, 역시 비위가 상해서 못 먹겠더라고요.

I can't eat uncooked food like raw fish or raw beef. I have tried to force myself to eat it before, but just as I thought, my stomach couldn't take it, so I couldn't eat it.

Study Notes

회 raw fish
익히다 to cook, to boil
먹다 to eat
억지로 by force
-(으)려고 in order to
시도하다 to try, to attempt
-아/어/여 보다 to try + V-ing
-(으)ㄴ 적(이) 있다 to have + V-ed (experience)
역시 also, as well, of course, as expected
비위가 상하다 to be displeased (with food), to find somet[h]

육회 raw beef
음식 food

- **Sample Dialogue**: For those who want to study how the conversation can be continued in Korean after one simple question and answer, a sample dialogue is provided using one of the previously introduced "Similar Questions".

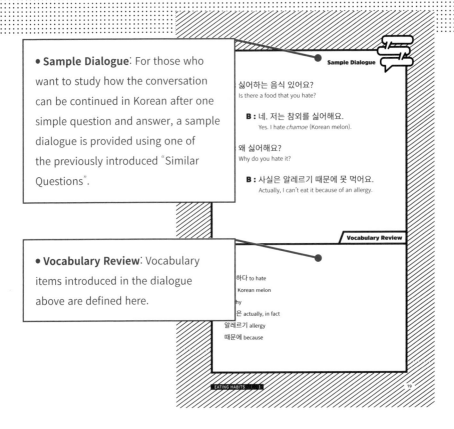

Sample Dialogue

싫어하는 음식 있어요?
Is there a food that you hate?

B : 네. 저는 참외를 싫어해요.
Yes. I hate *chamoe* (Korean melon).

왜 싫어해요?
Why do you hate it?

B : 사실은 알레르기 때문에 못 먹어요.
Actually, I can't eat it because of an allergy.

Vocabulary Review

- **Vocabulary Review**: Vocabulary items introduced in the dialogue above are defined here.

하다 to hate
Korean melon
hy
은 actually, in fact
알레르기 allergy
때문에 because

EATING HABITS　1　　　19

- **My Answers**: At the end of each category, a blank page is provided where you can write your own answers to the five main questions which you have learned. Please write only in Korean so that you can test yourself!

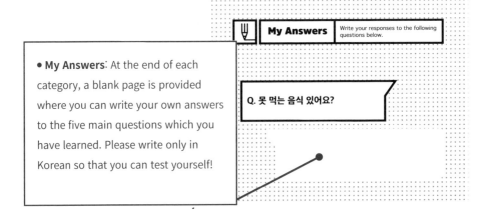

My Answers　Write your responses to the following questions below.

Q. 못 먹는 음식 있어요?

A large part of speaking Korean well is knowing how to answer certain questions and learning to anticipate the type of questions you may be asked in specific situations. This book will help you get accustomed to the most common sentence patterns used in questions, and the most typical ways to answer such questions.

There is no right or wrong way to study with this book because each person learns in a different way. Whether you prefer to study every page from cover to cover, or use it as an "as-needed" reference book whenever you need to practice on a specific topic, we at TTMIK suggest that you first read the "Main Question" to see if you can answer it in your own words, as well as come up with other ways to ask the question. Take some time to study the "Similar Questions" and "Sample Answers" in conjunction with the "TTMIK Teacher Answer" to learn various ways questions are asked and answered. Once you are well-versed with the aforementioned, use the short "Sample Dialogue" to become more familiar with the flow of a natural conversation in Korean. Finally, use the "My Answers" section to quiz yourself!

When studying with this book, our goal is for you to become more comfortable and confident when asking and answering varying questions in Korean. This will improve the flow of your conversations in Korean and develop your ability to give a more explicit response.

We hope you enjoy studying with the book, and please always make sure to actively ask questions and try to form different answers each time you talk with someone in Korean!

CONTENTS

YOUR THOUGHTS ABOUT WORK 직업관

YOUR TASTE IN DRAMA 드라마 취향

YOUR THOUGHTS ABOUT DATING 연애관

CELEBRITIES 연예인 / 유명인

PERSONALITIES 성격

SPENDING HABITS 소비 습관

OBSESSION, ADDICTION, COMPULSION 집착 / 중독 / 강박

1.
EATING
HABITS

못 먹는 음식 있어요?

Is there a food that you can't eat?

Similar Questions

싫어하는 음식 있어요?

Is there a food that you hate?

먹지 못하는 음식 있어요?

Is there a food that you can't eat?

알레르기 때문에 못 먹는 음식 있어요?

Is there a food that you can't eat because of an allergy?

Key Grammar Point

-는

Verb stem + -는 + Noun = Noun that + S + V

Ex) 좋아하다 + 책

⇨ 좋아하는 책 = **a book that (you) like**

네. 저는 (회)을/를 못 먹어요.

Yes. I can't eat (raw fish).

More Answers

저는 알레르기 때문에 (견과류)을/를 못 먹어요.
I can't eat (nuts) because of an allergy.

못 먹진 않지만 (해산물)을/를 굉장히 싫어해요.
It's not that I can't eat it, but I really hate (seafood).

아니요. 못 먹는 음식 없어요.
No. There is no food that I can't eat.

Vocabulary Review

먹다 to eat

음식 food

때문에 because of

굉장히 very, extremely

없다 to be not, to not have

싫어하다 to hate

알레르기 allergy

회 raw fish

견과류 nuts

못 먹는 음식 있어요?

Kyung-hwa's Answer

저는 회나 육회처럼 익히지 않은 음식은 못 먹어요. 억지로라도 먹어 보려고 시도해 본 적이 있는데, 역시 비위가 상해서 못 먹겠더라고요.

I can't eat uncooked food like raw fish or raw beef. I have tried to force myself to eat it before, but just as I thought, my stomach couldn't take it, so I couldn't eat it.

Study Notes

회 raw fish

익히다 to cook, to boil

먹다 to eat

억지로 by force

-(으)려고 in order to

시도하다 to try, to attempt

-아/어/여 보다 to try + V-ing

-(으)ㄴ 적(이) 있다 to have + V-ed (experience)

역시 also, as well, of course, as expected

비위가 상하다 to be displeased (with food), to find something disgusting to eat

육회 raw beef

음식 food

A : 싫어하는 음식 있어요?
Is there a food that you hate?

B : 네. 저는 참외를 싫어해요.
Yes. I hate *chamoe* (Korean melon).

A : 왜 싫어해요?
Why do you hate it?

B : 사실은 알레르기 때문에 못 먹어요.
Actually, I can't eat it because of an allergy.

Vocabulary Review

싫어하다 to hate

참외 Korean melon

왜 why

사실은 actually, in fact

알레르기 allergy

때문에 because

밥 양이 많은 편이에요?

Do you tend to eat a lot?

Similar Questions

밥 양이 남보다 많은 편이에요?

Do you tend to eat more than others?

밥을 많이 먹는 편이에요?

Do you tend to eat a lot?

식사량이 많은 편이에요?

Do you tend to have a lot to eat?

Key Grammar Point

-(으)ㄴ/는 편이다

Verb stem + -(으)ㄴ/는 편이다 = to tend to + V / to often + V

Ex) 바쁘다 + -(으)ㄴ/는 편이다

⇨ 바쁜 편이다 = **to be rather busy, to be usually busy**

네. 저는 밥 양이 많은 편이에요.

Yes. I tend to eat a lot.

More Answers

네. 저는 많이 먹는 편이에요.
Yes. I tend to eat a lot.

아니요. 저는 밥 양이 적은 편이에요.
No. I tend to eat small amounts.

아니요. 저는 조금 먹는 편이에요.
No. I tend to not eat a lot.

Vocabulary Review

밥 meal, food, rice

양 amount, quantity

-(으)ㄴ/는 편이다 to tend to, usually + V

남 others

많다 to be a lot

먹다 to eat

식사량 amount of food

적다 to be few/little

조금 a little bit

밥 양이 많은 편이에요?

Seokjin's Answer

저는 보통 끼니마다 밥을 한 주걱 반 정도 퍼서 먹어요. 이 정도면 밥그릇 밖으로 밥이 나올 정도는 아니기 때문에 많은 편은 아닌 것 같아요.

Every meal, I usually scoop up about one and a half rice paddles (servings) of rice. This amount of rice doesn't rise above the bowl, so I think I don't eat a lot.

Study Notes

보통 usually

-마다 every, each

주걱 rice paddle

정도 level, degree, approximately

먹다 to eat

밖 outside

때문에 because of

많다 to be a lot

-(으)ㄴ/는 편이다 to tend to; would usually + V

끼니 meal

밥 meal, food, rice

반 half

푸다 to scoop, to ladle

밥그릇 rice bowl

나오다 to come out

A : 밥을 많이 먹는 편이에요?

Do you tend to eat a lot?

B : 네. 밥 양이 많은 편이에요.

Yes, I tend to eat a lot.

A : 밥 많이 먹으면 몸에 안 좋아요. 양을 조금 줄여 보세요.

If you eat a lot, it's not good for your body. Try reducing the amount you eat.

B : 네. 줄여 볼게요.

Okay. I will try to reduce it.

Vocabulary Review

밥 meal, food, rice

많이 a lot

먹다 to eat

양 amount, quantity

-(으)ㄴ/는 편이다 to tend to; would usually + V

몸에 안 좋다 to be not good for health

조금 a little bit

줄이다 to decrease, to lower, to reduce

-아/어/여 보다 to try + -ing

아침은 꼭 먹는 편이에요?

Do you make sure you eat breakfast?

Similar Questions

아침을 챙겨 먹는 편이에요?

Do you make an effort to have breakfast?

아침은 꼭 먹고 다니는 편이에요?

Do you make sure you have breakfast before you start the day?

아침을 꼭 먹는 타입이에요?

Are you the type of person who must eat breakfast?

Key Grammar Point

꼭

꼭 + Verb = to make sure + S + V

Ex) 꼭 + 보다

⇨ 꼭 보세요. = Be sure to watch it.

네. 저는 아침은 꼭 먹는 편이에요.

Yes. I usually make sure I eat breakfast.

More Answers

네. 저는 아침을 꼭 먹고 다니는 편이에요.

Yes. I usually make sure I have breakfast.

아니요. 저는 아침 잘 안 먹어요.

No. I don't eat breakfast often.

아니요. 저는 아침 안 먹고 다녀요.

No. I don't eat breakfast on a daily basis.

Vocabulary Review

아침 morning, breakfast

꼭 to make sure + S + V; to be sure to + V

-(으)ㄴ/는 편이다 to tend to, usually + V

챙겨 먹다 to eat without missing a meal

먹고 다니다 to usually eat, to eat something on a daily basis

아침은 꼭 먹는 편이에요?

Jooyeon's Answer

아니요. 저는 아침을 챙겨 먹는 편은 아니에요. 아침에 일어나서 한 시간 정도는 아무것도 먹고 싶지 않아서 먹지 않기도 하지만 보통은 아침에 시간이 없어서 잘 못 먹어요.

No. I don't eat breakfast regularly. I don't eat breakfast because I don't want to eat anything until about 1 hour after I get up in the morning, but I often can't have it because I usually don't have time.

Study Notes

아침 morning, breakfast

챙겨 먹다 to eat without missing a meal

일어나다 to wake up

시간 time

정도 level, degree, approximately

아무것도 nothing

-고 싶다 to want to + V

-기도 하지만 to sometimes also + V +, but; it is true that S + V + but

보통 usually

없다 to be not, to not have

A : 아침을 챙겨 먹는 편이에요?

Do you tend not to skip breakfast?

B : 네. 아침은 꼭 챙겨 먹어요.

Yes. I always make sure I have breakfast.

A : 아침에 뭐 먹어요?

What do you have for breakfast?

B : 우유에 시리얼 타서 먹어요.

I put milk in cereal and eat it.

Vocabulary Review

아침 morning, breakfast

챙겨 먹다 to eat without missing a meal

-(으)ㄴ/는 편이다 to tend to; would usually + V

꼭 to make sure + S + V; to be sure to + V

우유 milk

시리얼 cereal

타서 먹다 to mix in (something) and eat

4 Q

외식을 자주 하는 편이에요?

Do you tend to eat out a lot?

Similar Questions

밖에서 자주 먹는 편이에요?

Do you often go out to eat?

집 밥을 자주 먹는 편이에요?

Do you often have meals at home?

밥을 자주 사 먹는 편이에요?

Do you tend to eat out often?

Key Grammar Point

자주

자주 + Verb = to + Verb + often

Ex) 자주 + 만나다

⇨ 자주 만나다 = **to meet often**

네. 저는 외식을 자주 하는 편이에요.

Yes. I tend to eat out often.

More Answers

네. 저는 밖에서 자주 사 먹는 편이에요.
Yes. I tend to eat out often.

아니요. 집에서 주로 먹어요.
No. I mainly eat at home.

아니요. 주로 집에서 해 먹는 편이에요.
No. I tend to mainly cook and eat at home.

Vocabulary Review

외식 eating out
자주 often
-(으)ㄴ/는 편이다 to tend to, usually + V
밖 outside
사 먹다 to buy and eat
집 house
주로 mainly
해 먹다 to cook and eat

외식을 자주 하는 편이에요?

Hyeonjeong's Answer

네. 자취를 한 이후로는 자주 외식하는 편이에요. 그런데 건강에는 좋지 않아서 음식 만드는 것을 배우려고 해요.

Yes. Ever since I started living on my own, I've eaten out often. But it's not good for my health, so I am going to learn how to cook.

Study Notes

자취 living on one's own away from family

이후 after

자주 often

외식 eating out

건강 health

좋다 to be good

음식 food

만들다 to make

배우다 to learn

-(으)려고 하다 to plan to + V

A : 외식을 자주 하는 편이에요?
Do you eat out often?

B : 아니요. 집에서 먹는 걸 좋아해요.
No. I like to eat at home.

A : 요리하는 거 좋아해요?
Do you like to cook?

B : 아니요. 주로 시켜 먹어요.
No. I mainly order delivery.

Vocabulary Review

외식 eating out
집 house
좋아하다 to like
주로 mainly
시켜 먹다 to order food delivery and eat it

자주 often
먹다 to eat
요리하다 to cook

규칙적인 식사를 하는 편이에요?

Do you tend to eat regular meals?

Similar Questions

규칙적으로 식사하는 편이에요?

Do you eat regularly?

식사 시간이 매일 비슷한 편이에요?

Are your meal times generally similar every day?

식사 시간이 매일 비슷해요?

Are your meal times similar every day?

Key Grammar Point

-적인 & -적으로

Many adjectives that end in -적인 can be converted to their adverb form by changing the end -적인 to -적으로.

Ex) 습관적인 (habitual) ⇨ 습관적으로 (habitually)

공격적인 (aggressive) ⇨ 공격적으로 (aggressively)

네. 저는 규칙적인 식사를 하는 편이에요.

Yes. I tend to eat regular meals.

More Answers

네. 식사 시간이 매일 비슷한 편이에요.
Yes. My meal times are generally similar every day.

아니요. 규칙적인 식사를 못 하고 있어요.
No. I don't eat regularly.

아니요. 매일 식사 시간이 다른 편이에요.
No. My meal times tend to be different every day.

Vocabulary Review

규칙적이다 to be regular
식사 meal
-(으)ㄴ/는 편이다 to tend to, usually + V
시간 time
매일 every day
비슷하다 to be similar
다르다 to be different

규칙적인 식사를 하는 편이에요?

Kyeong-eun's Answer

평일에는 규칙적인 식사를 하는 편이에요. 회사에서는 점심을 거의 한 시에 먹는 편이고 저녁도 보통 일곱 시쯤에 먹어요. 그렇지만 주말에는 외출을 많이 해서 규칙적으로 먹지는 못해요.

I tend to eat regularly on weekdays. At my company, I usually eat lunch at one o'clock, and I usually eat dinner at seven o'clock. However on weekends, I go out a lot, so I can't eat regularly.

Study Notes

평일 weekday

식사 meal

점심 lunch

저녁 dinner

보통 usually

쯤 about, around

그렇지만 but, however

주말 weekend

외출 going out

많이 a lot

규칙적이다 to be regular

회사 company

거의 almost

A : 식사 시간이 매일 비슷해요?

Are your meal times similar every day?

B : 네. 매일 비슷한 편이에요.

Yes. They tend to be similar every day.

A : 그럼 점심은 주로 한 시에 먹어요?

Then do you usually have lunch at one o'clock?

B : 네. 맞아요. 어떻게 알았어요?

Yes, that's right. How did you know?

Vocabulary Review

식사 meal

매일 every day

그럼 then

주로 mainly

먹다 to eat

맞다 to fit, to match, to be right

어떻게 how

알다 to know

시간 time

비슷하다 to be similar

점심 lunch

My Answers

Write your responses to the following questions below.

Q. 못 먹는 음식 있어요?

Q. 밥 양이 많은 편이에요?

Q. 아침은 꼭 먹는 편이에요?

Q. 외식을 자주 하는 편이에요?

Q. 규칙적인 식사를 하는 편이에요?

2.
SLEEPING
HABITS

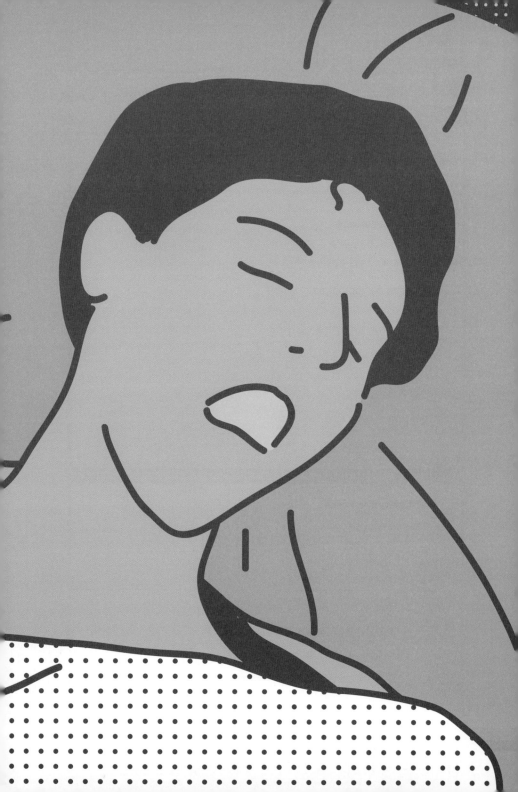

보통 몇 시 정도에 자요?

Around what time do you usually go to bed?

Similar Questions

보통 몇 시에 자요?

What time do you normally sleep?

보통 몇 시에 잠자리에 들어요?

What time do you normally go to bed?

밤에 몇 시에 자요?

What time do you sleep at night?

Key Grammar Point

보통 몇 시에

보통 = **usually, normally, generally**

몇 시에 = **at what time**

⇨ 보통 몇 시에 = **What time do you usually ...?**

보통 (한) 시 정도에 자요.

I normally go to bed around (one) o'clock.

More Answers

보통 (열) 시에 자요.
I normally go to bed at (ten) o'clock.

보통 (한) 시 정도에 누워요.
I normally lie down at (one) o'clock.

보통 (두) 시 정도에 잠자리에 들어요.
I normally go to bed around (two) o'clock.

Vocabulary Review

보통 usually

몇 시 what time

정도 level, degree, approximately

자다 to sleep

잠자리에 들다 to go to bed

밤 night

눕다 to lie (down)

보통 몇 시 정도에 자요?

Kyung-hwa's Answer

저는 자정 넘어서 자는 경우가 많아요. 일찍 자고 일찍 일어나는 습관을 들이고 싶은데, 막상 일찍 자려고 하면 하루를 일찍 끝내는 것 같아서 아쉽더라고요.

I often sleep after midnight. I want to get into the habit of going to bed early and waking up early, but when I actually try to go to bed early, I feel like I'm ending my day too early.

Study Notes

자정 midnight

자다 to sleep

많다 to be a lot

일어나다 to wake up

습관을 들이다 to form a habit

막상 in the event; when S + is actually about to + V

-(으)려고 하다 to plan to + V

하루 one day

끝내다 to finish

아쉽다 to be such a pity

넘다 to be past (a certain hour)

경우 case

일찍 early

A : 보통 몇 시에 자요?
What time do you normally go to bed?

B : 보통 한 시쯤에 자요.
I normally go to bed around one o'clock.

A : 늦게 자는 편이네요.
You go to bed rather late.

B : 네.
Yes.

Vocabulary Review

보통 usually

몇 시 what time

자다 to sleep

쯤 about, around

늦게 late

-(으)ㄴ/는 편이다 to tend to; would usually + V

하루에 보통 몇 시간 자요?

How many hours a day do you usually sleep?

Similar Questions

하루에 몇 시간 자요?

How many hours a day do you sleep?

하루에 얼마나 자요?

How much do you sleep a day?

밤에 몇 시간 자요?

How much do you sleep at night?

Key Grammar Point

하루에 몇 시간

하루 = **day**

-에 = **at, in**

몇 시간 = **how many hours**

⇨ 하루에 몇 시간 = **How many hours a day ...?**

하루에 보통 (여섯) 시간 자요.

I usually sleep (six) hours a day.

More Answers

보통 하루에 (일곱) 시간 자요.
I normally sleep (seven) hours a day.

보통 하루에 (여덟) 시간 정도 자요.
I normally sleep (eight) hours a day.

평균적으로 (아홉) 시간 정도 자요.
I sleep about (nine) hours on average.

Vocabulary Review

하루 one day
보통 usually
얼마나 how (much)
밤 night
평균적으로 on average
정도 level, degree, approximately

하루에 보통 몇 시간 자요?

Seokjin's Answer

하루에 보통 8시간 자요. 평소 일찍 자고 일찍 일어나는 습관이 있어서 저녁 10시쯤 되면 잠을 자고, 다음 날 아침 6시가 되면 잠에서 깨요.

I normally sleep 8 hours a day. I have a habit of usually going to bed early and waking up early, so I go to bed around 10 in the evening and wake up the next day at 6 in the morning.

Study Notes

하루 one day

시간 time

평소 usual times, usually, normally

자다 to sleep

습관 habit

저녁 dinner

잠을 자다 to sleep

다음 날 next day

아침 morning

깨다 to wake up

보통 usually

자다 to sleep

일찍 early

일어나다 to get up

A : 하루에 보통 몇 시간 자요?

How many hours do you normally sleep a day?

B : 보통 다섯 시간 자요. 하림 씨는요?

I normally sleep five hours. How about you, Ha-rim?

A : 저는 보통 열두 시간 자요.

I normally sleep 12 hours.

B : 진짜 많이 자네요.

You really sleep a lot.

Vocabulary Review

하루 one day

보통 usually

몇 시간 how many hours, a few hours

자다 to sleep

진짜 really, very, so

많이 a lot

아무 데서나 잘 자는 편이에요?

Can you normally sleep well just about anywhere?

Similar Questions

집이 아닌 곳에서도 잘 자는 편이에요?

Can you normally sleep well in a place that is not your house?

잠자리가 바뀌어도 잘 자는 편이에요?

Can you normally sleep well, even at a new location?

언제 어디에서나 잘 자는 편이에요?

Can you normally sleep well whenever and wherever?

Key Grammar Point

아무 데서나

아무(나) = **any, whichever**

데 = **place, spot**

-에서 = **at**

⇨ 아무 데서나 = **wherever, in any place, no matter where**

네. 아무 데서나 잘 자는 편이에요.

Yes. I normally sleep well just about anywhere.

More Answers

네. 언제 어디에서나 잘 자는 편이에요.
Yes. I tend to sleep well just about anywhere.

아니요. 집이 아닌 곳에서는 잘 못 자는 편이에요.
No. I normally can't sleep well in a place that is not my house.

아니요. 잠자리가 바뀌면 잘 못 자는 편이에요.
No. If my sleeping place changes, I normally can't sleep well.

Vocabulary Review

아무 데서나 anywhere
집 house
곳 place, spot
잠자리 bed, place to sleep
바뀌다 to be changed
언제 when

아무 데서나 잘 자는 편이에요?

Jooyeon's Answer

네. 저는 아무 데서나 잘 자는 편이에요. 예민한 편이 아니라서 정말 춥거나 불편한 곳이 아니라면 어디에서도 똑같이 잘 자는 것 같아요.

Yes. I usually sleep well just about anywhere. I am not that sensitive, so if it's not really cold or uncomfortable, I think I sleep equally well anywhere.

Study Notes

아무 데서나 anywhere

-(으)ㄴ/는 편이다 to tend to, would usually + V

예민하다 to be sensitive

정말 really

춥다 to be cold

불편하다 to be uncomfortable

곳 place

똑같다 to be the same, to be equal

A : 잠자리가 바뀌어도 잘 자는 편이에요?

Do you sleep well even if you are in a different place?

B : 네. 아무 데서나 잘 자는 편이에요.

Yes. I tend to sleep well just about anywhere.

A : 설마 영화관에서도 자는 거 아니죠?

Surely you don't sleep in movie theaters too, do you?

B : 아, 사실 영화관에서도 잘 자요.

Oh, actually, I sleep well in movie theaters, too.

Vocabulary Review

잠자리 bed, place to sleep

바뀌다 to be changed, to change

잘 well

아무 데서나 anywhere

설마 surely + S + won't + V; it is doubtful that S + V

영화관 movie theater

사실 fact, truth, actually

-도 also

Q

작은 소리에도 잘 깨는 편이에요?

Do even the slightest sounds easily wake you up?

Similar Questions

조그만 소리에도 잘 깨는 편이에요?

Do you normally wake up easily, even from low (volume) sounds?

조금만 소리 나도 잘 깨는 편이에요?

Do you normally wake up easily, even if a little sound is made?

작은 소리에도 쉽게 깨는 편이에요?

Do you tend to be easily woken up by soft sounds?

Key Grammar Point

-에도

-에 = **at, to**

-도 = **also**

⇨ -에도 = **even at, (reacting) even to**

네. 작은 소리에도 잘 깨는 편이에요.

Yes. I tend to wake up easily, even from soft sounds.

More Answers

네. 조금만 소리 나도 잘 깨는 편이에요.

Yes. I tend to wake up easily, even from small sounds.

아니요. 예민하지 않은 편이에요.

No. I am usually not that sensitive.

아니요. 큰 소리가 나도 잘 자는 편이에요.

No. I usually sleep well even when loud sounds are made.

Vocabulary Review

작은 small

소리 sound

깨다 to wake up

조그만 small, little, tiny

소리(가) 나다 to sound, a sound is made

예민하다 to be sensitive

큰 big

작은 소리에도 잘 깨는 편이에요?

Hyeonjeong's Answer

보통 때는 소리가 나는 줄도 모르고 자요. 가끔 많이 피곤한 날은 작은 소리에도 잠에서 깨게 돼요.

Usually, I sleep without noticing if there is any noise. Yet sometimes when I am very tired, I wake up even at the slightest sound.

Study Notes

보통 usually

소리가 나다 to sound

자다 to sleep

가끔 sometimes

피곤하다 to be tired

날 day

작은 small

소리 sound

깨다 to wake

-게 되다 to get to + V-ing

때 the time, the moment

모르다 to not know

A : 조금만 소리 나도 잘 깨는 편이에요?

Do you normally wake up easily even from the slightest sound?

B : 아니요. 저는 잘 때는 누가 업어 가도 몰라요.

No. When I sleep, even if someone carried me on their back, I wouldn't know.

A : 그럼 알람 소리는 어떻게 들어요?

Then how do you hear your alarm?

B : 알람 소리도 못 들어서 지각을 자주 하는 편이에요.

I can't hear my alarm either, so I am often late.

Vocabulary Review

조금만 just a little bit

깨다 to wake

알람 alarm

듣다 to listen

지각 being late, lateness, tardiness

자주 often

업어 가다 to carry someone on one's back, to piggyback someone

소리가 나다 to sound

모르다 to not know

소리 sound

잠이 잘 안 올 때는 보통 무엇을 해요?

What do you normally do when you can't sleep?

Similar Questions

잠이 잘 안 올 때는 무엇을 해요?

What do you do when you can't sleep?

잠이 잘 안 올 때는 어떻게 해요?

How do you cope when you can't sleep well?

잠이 잘 안 오면 어떻게 해요?

If you can't sleep well, what do you do?

Key Grammar Point

-(으)ㄹ 때

Verb stem + -(으)ㄹ 때 = when + S + V, if + S + V

Ex) 피곤하다 + -(으)ㄹ 때
⇨ 피곤할 때 = **when you are tired**

잠이 잘 안 올 때는 보통 (음악을 들)아/어/여요.

When I can't sleep, I normally (listen to music).

More Answers

잠이 잘 안 오면 보통 (우유를 마시)아/어/여요.
When I can't sleep, I normally (drink milk).

잠이 올 때까지 (책을 읽)아/어/여요.
I (read books) until I feel sleepy.

잠이 잘 안 와도 계속 누워 있어요.
I keep lying there even if I can't fall asleep easily.

Vocabulary Review

잠이 안 오다 can't sleep

무엇 what

어떻게 how, what

우유 milk

-까지 until

읽다 to read

-아/어/여도 even if, even though, even by + V-ing

누워 있다 to lie (down), to be lying down

보통 usually

하다 to do

음악을 듣다 to listen to music

마시다 to drink

책 book

계속 continuously, consecutively

잠이 잘 안 올 때는 보통 무엇을 해요?

Kyeong-eun's Answer

잠이 잘 안 올 때는 보통 음악을 들어요. 시끄러운 음악보다는 조용한 음악을 듣는 편이에요. 조용한 음악을 틀어 놓고 침대에 누워서 그 음악을 듣다 보면 잠이 올 때가 많아요.

When I can't sleep, I usually listen to quiet music. I tend to listen to quiet music rather than loud music. If I play quiet music, lie in my bed and listen to it, I find that I often fall asleep.

Study Notes

보통 usually

음악을 듣다 to listen to music

시끄럽다 to be loud, to be noisy

조용하다 to be quiet

틀어 놓다 to turn on; to keep something on

침대 bed

눕다 to lie (down)

-다 보면 if S + V; S will find that ..., after V-ing for a while; S will get to ...

잠이 오다 to get sleepy

A : 잠이 잘 안 올 때는 어떻게 해요?
What do you do when you can't sleep?

B : 따뜻한 우유를 마셔요.
I drink warm milk.

A : 그래도 잠이 안 오면요?
And if you still can't sleep?

B : 그럼 지루한 책을 읽어요.
Then I read a boring book.

Vocabulary Review

잠이 오다 to get sleepy

우유 milk

그럼 then

책 book

따뜻하다 to be warm

마시다 to drink

지루하다 to be boring

읽다 to read

My Answers

Write your responses to the following questions below.

Q. 보통 몇 시 정도에 자요?

Q. 하루에 보통 몇 시간 자요?

Q. 아무 데서나 잘 자는 편이에요?

Q. 작은 소리에도 잘 깨는 편이에요?

Q. 잠이 잘 안 올 때는 보통 무엇을 해요?

3.
YOUR SCHOOL DAYS

어떤 학생이 되고 싶었어요?

What kind of student did you want to be?

Similar Questions

어떤 유형의 학생이 되고 싶었어요?

What type of student did you want to be?

어떤 학생이 부러웠어요?

What kind of students were you jealous of?

어떤 유형의 학생이 부러웠어요?

What type of students were you jealous of?

Key Grammar Point

-이/가 되고 싶다

Noun + -이/가 되고 싶다 = to want to become + Noun

Ex) 경찰관 + -이 되고 싶다

⇨ 경찰관이 되고 싶어요. **= I want to become a police officer.**

(친구들한테 인기가 많)(으)ㄴ/는 학생이 되고 싶었어요.

I wanted to become a student who (was popular among friends).

More Answers

(공부를 잘하)(으)ㄴ/는 학생이 항상 되고 싶었어요.

I always wanted to be a student (who studied well/whose grades were good).

(그림을 잘 그리)(으)ㄴ/는 학생을 부러워했었어요.

I was jealous of students (who could draw well).

(리더십이 있)(으)ㄴ/는 학생이 멋있어 보였어요.

I thought students (who had good leadership) were cool.

Vocabulary Review

학생 student	되다 to become
유형 type, category	부럽다 to be jealous, to be envious
친구들 friends	인기가 많다 to be popular
공부 study	잘하다 to do well
그림 drawing, painting	그리다 to draw
리더십 leadership	멋있다 to be cool
-아/어/여 보이다 to look like	
어떤 which, what kind of, some kind of	

어떤 학생이 되고 싶었어요?

Kyung-hwa's Answer

저는 아주 어렸을 때, 달리기 잘하는 친구가 그렇게 멋있어 보이더라고요. 운동회 하이라이트인 400m 계주에서 결승선을 맨 처음 통과하는 친구들이 부러웠어요.

When I was very little, I found my friends who could run well to be really cool. I was jealous of students who crossed the finish line first in the 400 meter dash - the highlight of sports day.

Study Notes

아주 very, extremely

달리기 running

친구 friend

멋있다 to be cool

하이라이트 highlight

결승선 goal line, finish line

맨 처음 (very) first

통과하다 to pass through, to go through

부럽다 to be jealous, to be envious

어리다 to be young

잘하다 to do well

그렇게 so, like that

운동회 sports day, field day

계주 relay race

Sample Dialogue

A : 어떤 유형의 학생이 되고 싶었어요?
What kind of student did you want to become?

B : 공부도 잘하고 인기도 많은 학생이 되고 싶었어요.
I wanted to be a student who got good grades and was popular.

A : 학교 다닐 때 인기 없었어요?
Were you not popular when you were in school?

B : 네. 없었어요.
No, I wasn't.

Vocabulary Review

어떤 which

학생 student

-고 싶다 to want to + V

잘하다 to do well

인기가 많다 to be popular

학교 school

다니다 to go (to a place regularly), to attend (regularly)

유형 type, category

되다 to become

공부 studying

어떤 과목을 가장 좋아했어요?

Which school subject did you like the most?

Similar Questions

어떤 과목을 가장 잘했어요?

Which school subject were you best at?

어떤 과목이 가장 좋았어요?

Which school subject did you like the most?

가장 좋아하는 과목은 뭐였어요?

What was your favorite school subject?

Key Grammar Point

어떤

어떤 + Noun = **what kind of** + Noun / **which** + Noun

Ex) 어떤 + 맛

⇨ 어떤 맛 = **which flavor/taste**

(미술)을/를 가장 좋아했어요.

I liked (art class) the most.

More Answers

저는 (물리)을/를 가장 좋아하고 잘했어요.
I liked (physics) the most and was best at it.

저는 (영어)을/를 가장 좋아했는데 잘 못 했어요.
I liked (English) the most, but I wasn't good at it.

저는 (국사) 과목을 가장 좋아했는데 성적은 별로 안 좋았어요.
I liked the subject (Korean history) the most, but my grades weren't
very good.

Vocabulary Review

과목 subject

좋아하다 to like

잘하다 to do well, to be good at

좋다 to be good, to like

물리 physics

잘 못 하다 to be poor at, to be unskillful at

국사 history class (lit. history of the country)

성적 grade

별로 not really, not particularly

가장 the most

가장 좋아하는 one's favorite

영어 English

어떤 과목을 가장 좋아했어요?

Seokjin's Answer

저는 영어를 가장 좋아했었어요. 다른 나라 언어를 배우는 것이 마치 미지의 세계를 알아 가는 것처럼 느껴졌기 때문에 영어를 좋아했었어요.

I liked English the most. Learning the language of other countries felt like getting to know an unknown world, so I liked English.

Study Notes

영어 English

좋아하다 to like

나라 country

배우다 to learn

미지의 unknown

세계 world

알아 가다 to get to know

느껴지다 to feel

때문에 because

가장 the most

다른 different, other

언어 language

마치 as if

A : 가장 좋아하는 과목은 뭐였어요?
What was your favorite school subject?

B : 저는 수학을 가장 좋아했어요.
I liked math the most.

A : 진짜요? 어떻게 수학을 좋아할 수가 있어요?
Really? How can you like math?

B : 수학이 얼마나 재밌는데요.
Come on, math is so much fun.

Vocabulary Review

가장 좋아하는 one's favorite + N

과목 school subject

수학 math

진짜 really, very, so

어떻게 how

얼마나 how much

재미있다 to be interesting

Q

특별히 싫어하는 과목이 있었어요?

Was there a school subject that you particularly hated?

Similar Questions

특별히 안 좋아하는 과목이 있었어요?

Was there a school subject that you particularly disliked?

특별히 못하는 과목이 있었어요?

Was there a school subject that you were particularly bad at?

가장 싫어하는 과목은 뭐였어요?

What was the school subject that you hated the most?

Key Grammar Point

특별히

특별히 + Verb = to + particularly + Verb
/ to + Verb + in particular

Ex) 특별히 + 어렵다

⇨ 특별히 어렵다 = **to be particularly difficult**

네. 저는 (수학)을/를 정말 싫어했어요.

Yes. I really hated (math).

More Answers

저는 (지리)이/가 너무 어려워서 싫었어요.

I hated (geography) because it was too difficult.

저는 (세계사) 과목을 가장 싫어했고 성적도 안 좋았어요.

I hated the subject (world history) the most, and my grades were also bad.

아니요. 특별히 싫어하는 과목은 없었어요.

No. There weren't any particular subjects that I hated.

Vocabulary Review

싫어하다 to hate

못하다 to be bad at

지리 geography

어렵다 to be difficult, to be hard

세계사 world history

없다 to be not, to not have

특별히 especially, specially, particularly

과목 subject

수학 math

성적 grade

특별히 싫어하는 과목이 있었어요?

Jooyeon's Answer

저는 지리 과목을 싫어했어요. 지리 수업이
지루하기도 했고 재미없는 내용들을 다 암기
해야 해서 정말 힘들었던 기억이 있어요.

I hated geography. The geography classes were
not only boring, but I also have memories of
really tough moments memorizing all those
uninteresting things.

Study Notes

지리 geography

과목 school subject

싫어하다 to hate

지루하다 to be boring

재미없다 to not be fun; to be boring

내용 content, text

암기하다 to memorize

힘들다 to be difficult, to be tough, to be hard

기억 memory

Sample Dialogue

A : 가장 싫어하는 과목은 뭐였어요?

What was the school subject that you hated the most?

B : 체육을 제일 싫어했어요. 음악이 제일 좋았고요.

I hated PE the most. I liked music the best.

A : 진짜요? 노래 못하지 않아요?

Really? Aren't you a terrible singer?

B : 저 노래 진짜 잘해요. 불러 볼까요?

I am really good at singing. Do you want me to sing?

Vocabulary Review

가장 the most

과목 school subject

제일 the best, the most

노래 song

진짜 really, very, so

부르다 to sing

-아/어/여 보다 to try + -ing

싫어하다 to hate

체육 PE, physical education

좋다 to be good, to like

못하다 to be bad at

잘하다 to do well

학원을 많이 다니는 학생이었어요?

Were you a student who went to a lot of private institutes?

Similar Questions

학원을 여러 개 다니는 학생이었어요?

Were you a student who went to several private institutes?

학원을 여러 군데 다니는 학생이었어요?

Were you a student who went to various private academies?

학원을 많이 다니는 편이었어요?

Did you go to a lot of cram schools?

Key Grammar Point

군데

군데 **is a counter for places, parts or spots.**

Ex) 열 + 군데 ⇨ 열 군데 = 10 places

네. 저는 학원을 많이 다니는 학생이었어요.

Yes. I was a student who went to a lot of private institutes.

More Answers

네. 저는 학원을 정말 여러 군데 다녔어요.
Yes. I really went to a lot of private institutes.

아니요. 저는 학원을 별로 안 다녔어요.
No. I didn't go to many private academies.

아니요. 저는 학원을 거의 안 다녔어요.
No. I rarely went to cram schools.

Vocabulary Review

학원 private educational institute, cram school

많이 a lot

다니다 to go (to a place regularly), to attend (regularly)

학생 student

여러 개 several (items/things)

군데 places

별로 not really, not particularly

거의 안 ~ seldom, hardly

학원을 많이 다니는 학생이었어요?

Hyeonjeong's Answer

아니요. 공부를 좋아하지 않는 학생이었기 때문에 그냥 학교에서 배우는 걸로 공부는 끝냈어요.

No. I was a student who didn't like studying, so what I just learned in school was the only form of studying I did.

Study Notes

공부 study

좋아하다 to like

학생 student

때문에 because

그냥 just

학교 school

배우다 to learn

끝내다 to finish

A : 학원을 여러 군데 다니는 학생이었어요?

Were you a student who went to a lot of private institutes?

B : 네. 저는 학원 진짜 많이 다녔어요.

Yes. I went to quite a lot of institutes.

A : 주로 어떤 학원 다녔어요?

What institute did you usually go to?

B : 모든 과목 학원을 다 다녔어요.

I went to all institutes for every school subject.

Vocabulary Review

학원 private educational institute, cram school

여러 군데 a lot of places, various places

다니다 to go (to a place regularly), to attend (regularly)

학생 student

진짜 really, very, so

많이 a lot

선생님을 이성으로 좋아해 본 적 있어요?

Have you ever liked a teacher (romantically)?
(lit. Have you ever liked a teacher as a man/woman?)

Similar Questions

선생님을 좋아해 본 적 있어요?

Have you ever liked a teacher?

선생님을 이성으로 느꼈던 적 있어요?

Have you ever been attracted to a teacher?
(lit. Have you ever considered a teacher as a man/woman?)

이성으로 좋아하는 선생님이 있었어요?

Was there a teacher who you liked romantically?

Key Grammar Point

-아/어/여 본 적 있다

Verb stem + -아/어/여 본 적 있다 = to have + Verb + -ed

Ex) 먹다 + -아/어/여 본 적 있다

⇨ 먹어 본 적 있어요. **(I have eaten it before.)**

네. (중학교) 때 (체육) 선생님을 이성으로 좋아했었어요.

Yes. In (middle school), I liked the (physical education) teacher.

More Answers

네. (고등학교) 때 (화학) 선생님을 이성으로 느꼈었어요.
Yes. I liked my (chemistry) teacher in (high school).

아니요. 선생님을 이성으로 좋아해 본 적은 없어요.
No. I've never liked a teacher romantically.

아니요. 선생님을 이성으로 느낀 적은 없어요.
No. I've never had feelings toward a teacher.

Vocabulary Review

선생님 teacher   이성으로 romantically

좋아하다 to like

-(으)ㄴ 적(이) 있다 to have + V-ed (experience)

느끼다 to feel

있다 to be, to have

중학교 middle school

체육 PE, physical education

화학 chemistry

선생님을 이성으로 좋아해 본 적 있어요?

Kyeong-eun's Answer

네. 고등학교 때 국사 선생님을 좋아했어요. 이성으로 좋아한 것인지 존경한 것인지 아직도 조금 헷갈리지만 그 선생님 수업 시간에는 졸지도 않고 열심히 공부했던 기억이 있어요.

Yes. I liked my Korean history teacher in high school. I am still a bit uncertain whether I liked him as a man or looked up to him, but I do remember not dozing off in his class and studying hard.

Study Notes

국사 history class (lit. history of the country)

좋아하다 to like

존경하다 to respect

조금 a little bit

수업 class

졸다 to doze off, to nod off

열심히 hard

공부하다 to study

기억 memory

선생님 teacher

이성 opposite sex

아직도 still, yet

헷갈리다 to be confused

시간 time

A : 선생님을 좋아해 본 적 있어요?
Have you ever liked a teacher?

B : 네. 교생 선생님을 진짜 좋아했었어요.
Yes. I really liked my student teacher.

A : 교생 실습 끝나고 따로 연락했었어요?
Did you personally contact the teacher after the training period?

B : 아니요. 용기가 없었어요.
No. I didn't have the courage.

Vocabulary Review

선생님 teacher

좋아하다 to like

-(으)ㄴ 적(이) 있다 to have + V-ed (experience)

교생 선생님 student teacher, trainee teacher

진짜 really, very, so

실습 practical exercise, practical training

끝나다 to finish

따로 separately, individually, particularly

연락하다 to contact, to call, to get hold of

용기 courage, bravery

없다 to be not, to not have

My Answers

Write your responses to the following questions below.

Q. 어떤 학생이 되고 싶었어요?

Q. 어떤 과목을 가장 좋아했어요?

Q. 특별히 싫어하는 과목이 있었어요?

Q. 학원을 많이 다니는 학생이었어요?

Q. 선생님을 이성으로 좋아해 본 적 있어요?

4.
YOUR
THOUGHTS
ABOUT WORK

직장을 옮겨 본 적 있어요?

Have you ever transferred jobs?

Similar Questions

다른 회사로 옮겨 본 적 있어요?
Have you ever moved to a different company?

직장을 옮겨 본 경험이 있어요?
Have you ever had any experience switching jobs?

직업을 바꿔 본 적 있어요?
Have you ever changed jobs?

Key Grammar Point

-아/어/여 본 경험이 있다

Verb stem + -아/어/여 본 경험이 있다 = to have + Verb + -ed

Ex) 사다 + -아/어/여 본 경험이 있다

⇨ 사 본 경험이 있어요. = I have bought it before.

네. 옮겨 본 적 있어요.

Yes. I have changed jobs before.

More Answers

네. (두) 번 옮겨 봤어요.
Yes. I have switched jobs (twice).

아니요. 옮겨 본 적 없어요.
No. I've never changed jobs.

아니요. 한 번도 안 옮겨 봤어요.
No. Not even once have I switched jobs.

Vocabulary Review

직장 job

옮기다 to move, to transfer

-(으)ㄴ 적(이) 있다 to have + V-ed (experience)

다른 different, other

회사 company

경험 experience

바꾸다 to change

한 번도 not even once

직장을 옮겨 본 적 있어요?

Kyung-hwa's Answer

네. 한 번 있어요. 대학교 마지막 학기가 끝나자마자 영어 학원에서 아이들을 가르치기 시작했는데, 정확히 7개월 꽉 채워서 일하고, **Talk To Me In Korean**의 식구가 되었답니다.

Yes. Once. As soon as my last semester of college ended, I started teaching kids in an English institute. I worked there for exactly seven full months, and (then) I became a member of Talk To Me In Korean.

Study Notes

대학교 university, college

학기 semester

-자마자 as soon as

학원 private educational institute

가르치다 to teach

정확히 exactly, precisely

채우다 to fill

식구 family

마지막 last

끝나다 to finish, to end

영어 English

아이들 kids

시작하다 to start, to begin

꽉 tightly, firmly

일하다 to work

되다 to become

A : 직장을 옮겨 본 경험이 있어요?
Have you ever changed jobs?

B : 네. 저는 벌써 두 번째 직장을 옮겼어요.
Yes. I have already changed jobs twice.

A : 왜요?
Why?

B : 저한테 맞는 일을 찾고 싶어서요.
Because I want to find work which suits me.

Vocabulary Review

직장 job

옮기다 to move, to transfer

-(으)ㄴ 적(이) 있다 to have + V-ed (experience)

경험 experience

벌써 already

두 번째 second

왜 why

맞다 to fit, to match, to be right

일 work

찾다 to look for, to search for

-고 싶다 to want to + V

자신의 전공과 관련된 일을 하고 있어요?

Are you doing work that is related to your major?

Similar Questions

자신의 전공을 살리는 일을 하고 있어요?

Are you working at a job where you are using your major?

자신의 전공을 살려서 일을 하고 있어요?

Are you using your major in your current job?

자신의 전공과 관련된 일을 선택했어요?

Did you choose a job that was related to your major?

Key Grammar Point

-와/과 관련된

-와/과 = with

관련되다 = to be related

⇨ Noun A + -와/과 관련된 + Noun B

= Noun B that is related to Noun A

네. 제 전공과 관련된 일을 하고 있어요.

Yes. I am doing work that is related to my major.

More Answers

네. 제 전공을 살려서 일을 하고 있어요.
Yes. I am using my major at my current job.

아니요. 제 전공과 관련이 없는 일을 하고 있어요.
No. I am doing work that is not related to my major.

아니요. 제 전공과 지금 하고 있는 일은 관련이 없어요.
No. My major and the work I am doing now are not related.

Vocabulary Review

자신 oneself

전공 major

관련된 related

일 work, job

하다 to do

전공을 살리다 to use one's major at work

선택하다 to choose, to select

자신의 전공과 관련된 일을 하고 있어요?

Seokjin's Answer

네. 저는 대학교 때 전공이 영어였는데, 현재 외국인들에게 한국어를 가르치는 일을 하고 있어요. 한국어 질문에 대한 답을 할 때나 문법을 설명할 때 주로 영어를 쓰고 있기 때문에 대학교 때 전공한 영어가 큰 도움이 되고 있어요.

Yes. My major in college was English, and I am currently doing work where I teach Korean to foreigners. When I answer questions about Korean or explain grammar, I use English, so my English major from college is a big help.

Study Notes

대학교 university, college	전공 major
영어 English	현재 current, the present
외국인 foreigner	가르치다 to teach
일 work, job	질문 question
답 answer	문법 grammar
설명하다 to explain	주로 mainly
쓰다 to use	때문에 because
큰 big	도움이 되다 to be helpful

A : 자신의 전공을 살려서 일을 하고 있어요?
Are you doing work that uses your major?

B : 아니요. 전혀 관련 없는 일을 하고 있
어요.
No. I am doing work that has nothing to do
with my major.

A : 전공이 뭐였는데요?
What was your major?

B : 경영학이요.
Business administration.

Vocabulary Review

자신 oneself

전공을 살리다 to use one's (college) major at work

일 work

전혀 not at all

관련 related, relation

경영학 business administration

직장 상사와 트러블을 겪었던 적 있어요?

Have you ever had trouble with your boss at work?

Similar Questions

직장 상사와 싸워 본 적 있어요?

Have you ever fought with your boss at work?

직장 상사와 문제가 있었던 적 있어요?

Have you ever had a problem with your boss at work?

직장 상사와 맞서 본 적 있어요?

Have you ever stood up to your boss at work?

Key Grammar Point

-았/었/였던 적(이) 있다

Verb stem + -았/었/였던 적(이) 있다 = to have + Verb + -ed

Ex) 아프다 + -았/었/였던 적(이) 있다

⇨ 아팠던 적 있어요. **= I have been sick before.**

네. 직장 상사와 트러블을 겪었던 적 있어요.

Yes. I have had trouble with my boss before.

More Answers

네. 직장 상사와 트러블이 있었던 적 있어요.
Yes. I have had trouble with my boss before.

아니요. 그런 적 없어요.
No. I haven't.

아니요. 직장 상사와 트러블을 겪었던 적은 없어요.
No. I have never had trouble with my boss before.

Vocabulary Review

직장 job, work place

상사 superior, boss

겪다 to experience, to undertake, to undergo

-(으)ㄴ 적(이) 있다 to have + V-ed (experience)

싸우다 to fight

문제 problem

맞서다 to stand against, to fight against

직장 상사와 트러블을 겪었던 적 있어요?

Jooyeon's Answer

아니요. 저는 일한 지 일 년밖에 안 되어서
그런지 직장 내 트러블 경험은 아직 없어요.

No. Maybe because it has only been one year
since I started working, so I haven't had any
trouble at work so far.

Study Notes

일하다 to work

-(으)ㄴ 지 ~ 되다 to have been (an amount of time) since

-밖에 only

직장 job

내 inside

경험 experience

아직 yet, still

A : 직장 상사와 맞서 본 적 있어요?

Have you ever confronted a superior at work?

B : 아니요. 왜요? 무슨 일 있어요?

No. Why? Did something happen?

A : 저희 회사 과장님이 자꾸 저한테 화를 내요.

The section chief at my company keeps getting angry at me.

B : 스트레스 많이 받겠어요.

It must be really stressful.
(lit. You must be getting a lot of stress.)

Vocabulary Review

직장 job

상사 superior, boss

맞서다 to stand against, to fight against

-(으)ㄴ 적(이) 있다 to have + V-ed (experience)

회사 company

과장님 manager, section chief

자꾸 over and over, repeatedly, often, keep doing something

화를 내다 to get angry, to show one's anger

받다 to get, to receive

부모님이 자신에게 기대했던 직업이 있어요?

Was there a profession that your parents expected you to have?

Similar Questions

부모님이 자신에게 강요한 직업이 있어요?

Was there a job that your parents compelled you to have?

부모님이 나에게 원했던 직업이 있어요?

Was there a job that your parents wanted you to have?

부모님이 나에게 바랐던 직업이 있어요?

Was there a job that your parents wanted for you?

Key Grammar Point

-에게 기대하다

-에게 = **to, toward, from**

기대하다 = **to expect**

⇨ **Person** + -에게 기대하다 = **to expect from + person**

네. 저희 부모님은 제가 (의사)이/가 되길 바라셨어요.

Yes. My parents wanted me to become (a doctor).

More Answers

네. 저희 부모님은 제가 (교육자)의 길을 가길 바라셨어요.
Yes. My parents wanted me to go on the path of becoming (an educator).

아니요. 없어요.
No. There was none.

아니요. 저희 부모님은 제가 하고 싶은 일을 하라고 하셨어요.
No. My parents told me to do whatever I wanted to do.

Vocabulary Review

부모님 parents

직업 job

원하다 to want

의사 doctor

교육자 educator, teacher

가다 to go

기대하다 to expect, to look forward to

자신 oneself

강요하다 to force

바라다 to hope, to want

되다 to become

길 way, road, route, path

-고 싶다 to want to + V

부모님이 자신에게 기대했던 직업이 있어요?

Hyeonjeong's Answer

딱히 그런 건 없으셨던 거 같아요. 그냥 회사에 들어가서 월급을 받았으면 좋겠다는 생각을 하신 것 같아요.

I don't think there was anything like that in particular. I think they just thought it would be nice if I could enter a company and get a salary.

Study Notes

딱히 nothing special, not in particular

그런 거 such thing

회사 company

들어가다 to go in, to start

월급 salary, monthly pay

받다 to get, to receive

생각하다 to think

A : 취업 축하해요. 부모님이 좋아하시겠어요.

Congratulations on getting a job. Your parents must be happy.

B : 감사합니다. 부모님은 사실 좀 실망하셨어요.

Thank you. My parents were actually a bit disappointed.

A : 왜요? 거기 좋은 회사인데.

Why? It's a good company.

B : 부모님은 제가 선생님이 되길 바라셨어요.

My parents wanted me to become a teacher.

Vocabulary Review

축하하다 to congratulate

좋아하시다 to like (honorific)

좀 a little bit, kind of

좋다 to be good, to like

선생님 teacher

바라다 to hope, to want

취업 employment, getting a job, finding a position

부모님 parents

사실 fact, truth, actually

실망하다 to be disappointed

회사 company

되다 to become

이 세상의 모든 직업 중에 하나를 선택할 수 있다면, 어떤 직업을 선택하고 싶어요?

If you could choose one out of all the jobs in the world, what would you want to choose?

Similar Questions

이 세상의 모든 직업 중에 하나를 고를 수 있다면, 어떤 직업을 선택하고 싶어요?
If you could choose one out of all the jobs in the world, what would you want to choose?

이 세상의 모든 직업을 가질 수 있다면, 어떤 직업을 선택하고 싶어요?
If you could have all the jobs in the world, which job would you want to choose?

이 세상의 어떤 직업도 가질 수 있다면, 어떤 직업을 선택하고 싶어요?
If you could choose any job in the world, which job would you choose?

Key Grammar Point

-(으)ㄹ 수 있다면

Verb stem + -(으)ㄹ 수 있다면 = if + S + could + V

Ex) 다시 하다 + -(으)ㄹ 수 있다면
= 다시 할 수 있다면 = **if you could do it again**

이 세상의 모든 직업 중에 하나를 선택할 수 있다면, 저는 (카레이서)을/를 선택하고 싶어요.

If I could choose one out of all the jobs in the world,
I would choose to be a/an (race car driver).

More Answers

그렇다면 저는 (영화감독)을/를 선택하고 싶어요.
Then, I would choose to be a/an (movie director).

제 마음대로 직업을 선택할 수 있다면 저는 (전투기 조종사)을/를
선택하고 싶어요.
If I could choose any job, I would choose to be a/an (fighter pilot).

이 세상의 모든 직업 중에 하나를 선택할 수 있다면, 저는 (가수)이/가
되고 싶어요.
If I could choose any job in the world, I want to be a/an (singer).

Vocabulary Review

세상 world
직업 job
선택하다 to choose, to select
-(으)면 if
고르다 to pick, to choose
어떤 which, what kind of, some kind of
영화 감독 movie director
가수 singer
마음대로 as one likes, to one's liking

모든 every, all
하나 one
-(으)ㄹ 수 있다 to be able to + V
-고 싶다 to want to + V
가지다 to have
카레이서 race car driver
전투기 조종사 fighter pilot
되다 to become

이 세상의 모든 직업 중에 하나를 선택할 수 있다면, 어떤 직업을 선택하고 싶어요?

Kyeong-eun's Answer

저한테는 너무 어려운 질문인 거 같아요. 어떤 직업이라도 힘든 점은 있을 거라고 생각하기 때문에 딱 떠오르는 직업이 없네요.

I think it is too difficult a question for me. I think any job would have difficult parts to it, so there is no specific job that comes to mind.

Study Notes

너무 so, really, too much

어렵다 to be difficult, to be hard

질문 question

직업 job

힘든 점 difficult thing, difficult part

생각하다 to think

딱 just, exactly

떠오르다 to rise, to come up

A : 이 세상의 모든 직업 중에 하나를 고를 수 있다면, 어떤 직업을 선택하고 싶어요?

If you could pick one job out of all the jobs in this world, what would you want to choose?

B : 저는 가수가 되고 싶어요.

I would want to be a singer.

A : 가수는 노래를 잘해야 할 수 있는 직업이에요.

A singer is a job that you can only have when you can sing well.

B : 저도 알아요.

I know that, too.

Vocabulary Review

세상 world

직업 job

고르다 to pick, to choose

어떤 which, some

가수 singer

노래 song

알다 to know

선택하다 to choose, to select, to decide

모든 every, all

하나 one

-(으)ㄹ 수 있다 to be able to + V

-고 싶다 to want to + V

되다 to become

My Answers

Write your responses to the following questions below.

Q. 직장을 옮겨 본 적 있어요?

Q. 자신의 전공과 관련된 일을 하고 있어요?

Q. 직장 상사와 트러블을 겪었던 적 있어요?

Q. 부모님이 자신에게 기대했던 직업이 있어요?

Q. 이 세상의 모든 직업 중에 하나를 선택할 수 있다면, 어떤 직업을 선택하고 싶어요?

5.
YOUR TASTE IN DRAMA

주로 어디서 드라마를 봐요?

Where do you normally watch dramas?

Similar Questions

주로 어디서 드라마를 보는 편이에요?
Where do you mainly watch dramas?

주로 어디서 드라마를 보게 돼요?
Where do you mainly get to watch dramas?

드라마는 보통 어디서 봐요?
Where do you normally watch dramas?

Key Grammar Point

주로

주로 = mainly, usually

Ex) 주로 언제 일어나요? = When do you normally get up?

주로 (제 방)에서 드라마를 봐요.

I usually watch dramas at/in (my room).

More Answers

저는 (지하철)에서 드라마를 많이 봐요.
I watch dramas in (the subway).

저는 주로 (회사)에서 봐요.
I mainly watch them at (my company).

(학교)에서 많이 봐요.
I watch them a lot at (school).

Vocabulary Review

주로 mainly
드라마 drama
보다 to watch, to see
-게 되다 to get to + V-ing
보통 usually
방 room
지하철 subway
많이 a lot
회사 company

주로 어디서 드라마를 봐요?

Kyung-hwa's Answer

저는 요즘 드라마는 거의 지하철에서 보는 것 같아요. 여기저기 이동할 때 틈틈이 핸드폰으로 보는데, 화질이 TV보다 떨어져서 참 아쉬워요.

I think I mostly watch dramas in the subway these days. When I am on the go, I watch them on my phone in my spare time, but it's too bad that the video quality isn't as good as on TV.

Study Notes

요즘 these days

지하철 subway

여기저기 here and there

틈틈이 in one's spare time

화질 image quality

-보다 than

떨어지다 to decrease, to drop; to be lower than the standard

참 really, very, so, quite

아쉽다 to be such a pity

-(으)ㄴ 것 같다 to look like, to seem like, one thinks that + S + V

거의 almost

보다 to see, to watch

이동하다 to move (location)

핸드폰 cell phone

A : 어제 시작한 드라마 봤어요?

Did you watch the drama that started yesterday?

B : 아니요. 지민 씨는 주로 어디서 드라마를 보는 편이에요?

No. Ji-min, where do you mainly watch your dramas?

A : 주로 퇴근길 지하철에서 봐요. 왜요?

I mainly watch them in the subway on my way home from work. Why?

B : 아, 핸드폰으로 보는구나. 아니, 지민 씨 되게 바빠 보이는데, 드라마를 다 챙겨 보는 것 같아서 궁금했어요.

Oh, you watch them on your phone. I mean, you look so busy, but you never seem to miss any dramas, so I was just wondering.

Vocabulary Review

어제 yesterday

보다 to see, to watch

퇴근길 one's way home from work

되게 very, so

보이다 to be seen, to seem, to show

챙겨 보다 to watch without missing an episode

궁금하다 to be curious

시작하다 to start, to begin

주로 mainly

지하철 subway

바쁘다 to be busy

Q

특별히 선호하는 드라마 장르가 있어요?

Is there a particular drama genre that you prefer?

Similar Questions

특별히 선호하는 드라마 장르는 어떤 장르예요?

What is a particular drama genre that you prefer?

특별히 좋아하는 드라마 장르가 있어요?

Is there a particular drama genre that you prefer?

특별히 선호하는 내용의 드라마가 있어요?

Is there a particular drama with a story that you prefer?

Key Grammar Point

-는 내용의

-는 = modifier

내용 = content, text

-의 = of

⇨ Verb stem + -는 내용의 = of which the story is + S + V

네. 저는 (정치) 드라마를 좋아해요.

Yes. I like (political) dramas.

More Answers

네. 저는 (사랑) 이야기만 좋아해요.

Yes. I only like stories about (love).

아니요. 특별히 선호하는 장르는 없어요.

No. There is no genre that I particularly prefer.

아니요. 특별히 좋아하는 장르는 없어요.

No. There is no genre that I like in particular.

Vocabulary Review

특별히 specially, particularly   정치 politics

선호하다 to prefer   사랑 love

장르 genre   이야기 story

좋아하다 to like   -만 only

내용 content, text

특별히 선호하는 드라마 장르가 있어요?

Seokjin's Answer

특별히 선호하는 장르는 없어요. 단, 제가 좋아하는 배우가 나오면 관심을 가지고 보는 편이에요. 그런데 제가 좋아하는 배우들은 다 나이가 많은 편이라서 요즘 TV 드라마에는 잘 안 나와요.

There is no particular genre that I prefer. Except when an actor I like is on a show, then I tend to watch with interest. But the actors I like are mostly old, so they don't appear in a lot of TV dramas these days.

Study Notes

단 but, however

좋아하다 to like

배우 actor, actress

나오다 to come out, to appear; to be released

관심 interest

갖다 to have, to own

보다 to see, to watch

-(으)ㄴ/는 편이다 to tend to; would usually + V

나이가 많다 to be old

요즘 these days

A : 요즘 재밌는 드라마 뭐 있어요?
What dramas are fun to watch these days?

B : 특별히 좋아하는 드라마 장르가 있어요?
Is there a genre of dramas that you particularly like?

A : 멜로도 좋아하고 액션도 좋아해요.
I like romantic dramas and also action dramas.

B : 아, 그렇구나. 요즘은 스릴러가 대세예요.
Oh, I see. These days, thrillers are all the rage.

Vocabulary Review

요즘 these days

재밌는 interesting

특별히 especially, specially, particularly

좋아하다 to like

장르 genre

멜로 (영화) romantic movie

액션 action

대세 general trend

가장 재밌게 본 드라마 제목이 뭐예요?

What is the title of the drama that you've enjoyed the most?

Similar Questions

가장 재밌게 본 드라마는 어떤 드라마예요?

Which drama did you enjoy the most?

가장 좋아하는 드라마는 어떤 드라마예요?

Which drama do you like the most?

가장 좋아하는 드라마 제목이 뭐예요?

What is the title of the drama you like the most?

Key Grammar Point

가장

가장 + adjective/adverb = **the most** + adjective/adverb

Ex) 가장 + 비싸다 = 가장 비싸요. = **It's the most expensive.**

제가 가장 재밌게 본 드라마는 ('별에서 온 그대')이에요/예요.

The drama that I've enjoyed the most is
("You Who Came from the Stars").

More Answers

제가 가장 좋아하는 드라마는 ('태양의 후예')이에요/예요.
My favorite drama is ("Descendants of the Sun").

저는 ('환상의 커플')을/를 가장 재밌게 봤어요.
I enjoyed ("The Fantastic Couple") the most.

('해를 품은 달')이/가 제가 가장 좋아하는 드라마예요.
("The Moon Embracing the Sun") is my favorite drama.

Vocabulary Review

가장 the most

보다 to watch, to see

가장 좋아하는 one's favorite

후예 descendant

커플 couple

달 moon

어떤 which, what kind of, some kind of

재미있다 to be interesting

제목 title

태양/해 sun

환상 fantasy, illusion

품다 to embrace

가장 재밌게 본 드라마 제목이 뭐예요?

Jooyeon's Answer

재밌게 본 드라마가 정말 많은데 그중에서 가장 재미있었던 걸 뽑자면 저는 '응답하라' 시리즈를 뽑을 것 같아요. 지금까지 총 세 편의 시리즈가 나왔는데 다 너무 재밌게 봤어요.

There are really a lot of dramas that I've enjoyed, and if I were to pick one that I've enjoyed the most, I would pick the "Reply..." series. So far there have been three seasons, and I've enjoyed all of them very much.

Study Notes

재미있다 to be interesting

많다 to be a lot

가장 the most

지금까지 until now

편 counter for movies/shows

너무 so, really, too much

나오다 to come out, to appear; to be released

-(으)ㄴ 것 같다 to look like, to seem like, one thinks that + S + V

정말 really

그중에서 among them

뽑다 to pick, to choose

총 total

다 every, all

보다 to see, to watch

A : 가장 좋아하는 드라마 제목이 뭐예요?
What is the title of your favorite drama?

B : '태양의 후예'요.
It's "Descendants of the Sun".

A : 주인공이 누구예요?
Who are the main characters?

B : 송중기랑 송혜교가 나와요.
Song Joong-ki and Song Hye-gyo are in it.

Vocabulary Review

가장 좋아하는 one's favorite + N

제목 title

주인공 main character

나오다 to come out, to appear, to be released

한국 드라마를 주로 봐요, 외국 드라마를 주로 봐요?

Do you mainly watch Korean dramas or foreign dramas?

Similar Questions

한국 드라마를 더 많이 봐요, 외국 드라마를 더 많이 봐요?

Do you watch Korean dramas or foreign dramas more often?

한국 드라마를 좋아해요, 외국 드라마를 좋아해요?

Do you like Korean dramas or foreign dramas?

한국 드라마랑 외국 드라마 중에 어떤 걸 더 많이 봐요?

Between Korean dramas and foreign dramas, which do you watch more often?

Key Grammar Point

중에

Noun + 중에 = among + Noun (plural)

Ex) 친구들 중에 = among my friends

저는 주로 (미국 드라마)을/를 많이 봐요.

I mainly watch a lot of (American dramas).

More Answers

저는 (한국 드라마)을/를 더 좋아해요.
I like (Korean dramas) better.

저는 (외국 드라마)을/를 더 많이 봐요.
I watch (foreign dramas) more.

저는 둘 다 많이 봐요.
I watch a lot of both.

Vocabulary Review

주로 mainly

외국 foreign country

많이 a lot

더 more

보다 to watch, to see

좋아하다 to like

미국 the USA

둘 다 both

한국 드라마를 주로 봐요, 외국 드라마를 주로 봐요?

Hyeonjeong's Answer

저는 찾아서 보는 드라마는 외국 드라마인데, 우연히 보게 되었다가 계속 시청하는 건 한국 드라마예요. 주로 누가 보고 있을 때 옆에서 보다가 빠져들게 되는데, 뻔한 스토리인데도 자꾸 보게 돼요.

The dramas that I actively look for and watch are foreign dramas, but the ones that I end up accidentally watching and continue to watch are Korean dramas. I usually just watch what someone else is watching and then fall into it, and even though the storyline is obvious, I can't stop watching them.

Study Notes

찾다 to look for, to search for

외국 foreign country

-게 되다 to get to + V-ing

시청하다 to watch

옆 side, next to

빠져들다 to get addicted to; to fall in love with

뻔하다 to be obvious, to be evident

자꾸 over and over, repeatedly, often

보다 to see, to watch

우연히 by accident

계속 continuously, consecutively

주로 mainly

-다가 while + V-ing

A : 한국 드라마를 더 많이 봐요, 외국 드라마를 더 많이 봐요?

Do you watch Korean dramas or foreign dramas more often?

B : 저는 외국 드라마를 더 많이 봐요.

I watch foreign dramas more often.

A : 외국 드라마 어떤 거요?

Which foreign dramas?

B : 저는 미드를 주로 보는 편이에요.

I usually watch American dramas.

한국 Korea

외국 foreign country

더 more

많이 a lot

보다 to see, to watch

주로 mainly

-(으)ㄴ/는 편이다 to tend to; would usually + V

미드 an acronym for '미'국 '드'라마, American dramas

드라마 보려고 일부러 일찍 집에 들어가 본 적 있어요?

Have you ever gone home early on purpose
in order to watch a drama?

Similar Questions

드라마 보려고 일부러 일찍 귀가해 본 적 있어요?

Have you ever gone home early on purpose in order to watch a drama?

드라마 때문에 일부러 일찍 집에 들어가 본 적 있어요?

Have you ever gone home early on purpose because of a drama?

드라마 보고 싶어서 일부러 일찍 집에 들어가 본 적 있어요?

Have you ever gone home early on purpose because you wanted to
watch a drama?

Key Grammar Point

-(으)려고

Verb stem + -(으)려고 = in order to + Verb / so that one can + V

Ex) 친구를 만나다 + -(으)려고

= 친구를 만나려고 **(in order to meet a friend)**

네. ('킬미, 힐미') 할 때 그거 보려고 일부러 일찍 집에 들어가곤 했어요.

Yes. I used to go home early on purpose when ("Kill Me, Heal Me") was airing.

More Answers

네. ('대장금') 할 때 그랬어요.
Yes. I did that when ("Dae Jang Geum") was airing.

아니요. 그런 적은 없어요.
No. I've never done that before.

아니요. 한 번도 그런 적은 없어요.
No. I haven't even done that once before.

Vocabulary Review

-(으)려고 in order to

일찍 early

들어가다 to go in

-고 싶다 to want to + V

한 번도 not once

-(으)ㄴ 적(이) 있다 to have + V-ed (experience)

귀가하다 to come home, to return home

일부러 on purpose

집 house

때문에 because of

-곤/고는 하다 would often + V

드라마 보려고 일부러 일찍 집에 들어가 본 적 있어요?

Kyeong-eun's Answer

네. 요즘에는 '태양의 후예'를 보려고 수요일, 목요일에 집에 일찍 들어가요. 드라마를 정말 좋아해서, 제가 좋아하는 드라마를 하면 일부러 일찍 집에 들어가서 본 적이 많아요.

Yes. These days, I go home early on Wednesdays and Thursdays to watch "Descendants of the Sun". I really like dramas, so I have gone home early on purpose many times when a drama that I liked was airing.

Study Notes

요즘 these days

후예 descendant, offspring

-(으)려고 in order to

목요일 Thursday

일찍 early

들어가다 to go in, to start

정말 really

좋아하다 to like

일부러 on purpose

-(으)ㄴ 적(이) 있다 to have + V-ed (experience)

태양 sun

보다 to see, to watch

수요일 Wednesday

집 house

A : 드라마 때문에 일부러 일찍 집에 들어가 본 적 있어요?

Have you ever gone home early on purpose because of a drama?

B : 네. 오늘 드라마 보러 집에 일찍 들어가야 돼요.

Yes. I have to go home early today to watch a drama.

A : 드라마 때문에 약속을 안 잡아요?

You don't make plans because of dramas?

B : 드라마 보려고 집에 일찍 들어가는 사람들 많아요.

There are many people who go home early to watch dramas.

Vocabulary Review

때문에 because of

일부러 on purpose

일찍 early

집 house

들어가다 to go in; to start

사람들 people

-(으)ㄴ 적(이) 있다 to have + V-ed (experience)

-(으)러 가다 to go + V-ing

-아/어/여야 돼다 should + V

약속을 잡다 to make an appointment, to arrange a meeting

-(으)려고 in order to

많다 to be a lot

My Answers

Write your responses to the following questions below.

Q. 주로 어디서 드라마를 봐요?

Q. 특별히 선호하는 드라마 장르가
있어요?

Q. 가장 재밌게 본 드라마 제목이 뭐예요?

Q. 한국 드라마를 주로 봐요, 외국 드라마를 주로 봐요?

Q. 드라마 보려고 일부러 일찍 집에 들어가 본 적 있어요?

6.
YOUR THOUGHTS ABOUT DATING

마음에 드는 사람에게 먼저 다가가는 편이에요?

If you like someone, are you usually the one
who approaches him/her first?

Similar Questions

마음에 드는 사람에게 적극적으로 다가가는 편이에요?

Do you tend to actively approach someone you like?

마음에 드는 사람에게 먼저 말을 거는 편이에요?

If you like someone, are you usually the one to talk to him/her first?

마음에 드는 사람이 생기면 먼저 다가가는 편이에요?

If you find someone you like, do you tend to approach him/her first?

Key Grammar Point

먼저

**먼저 + Verb = Verb + first/before the other person
/ to take the initiative to + Verb**

Ex) 먼저 + 가다 ⇨ 먼저 갈게요. = I will go first.

네. 저는 마음에 드는 사람에게 먼저 다가가는 편이에요.

Yes. When I like someone, I tend to approach him/her first.

More Answers

네. 저는 어떤 사람이 마음에 들면 먼저 다가가는 편이에요.
Yes. When I like someone, I tend to approach him/her first.

아니요. 저는 어떤 사람이 마음에 들어도 못 다가가는 편이에요.
No. Even when I like someone, I usually can't approach him/her.

아니요. 저는 어떤 사람이 마음에 들어도 적극적으로 표현하지 못하는 편이에요.
No. Even when I like someone, I usually can't actively express how I feel.

Vocabulary Review

마음에 들다 to be liked, to be liked, to like, to find something likeable

사람 person

먼저 first

다가가다 to approach, to come up to

적극적으로 actively, aggressively

말을 걸다 to initiate a conversation

생기다 to happen, to be formed, to be made

표현하다 to express

마음에 드는 사람에게 먼저 다가가는 편이에요?

Seokjin's Answer

네. 돌이켜 보면 마음에 드는 사람에게 제가 먼저 다가갔던 것 같아요. 주로 간식을 사 주면서 말을 걸거나, 따로 전화 연락을 하거나, 식사 약속을 잡아서 관심을 보였었어요.

Yes. Looking back, I think I have approached the people I like first. I usually started a conversation while buying them some snacks, called them in person, or showed my interest by arranging a dinner date with them.

Study Notes

돌이켜 보다 to reach back (in one's memories), to think about the past

-(으)ㄴ 것 같다 to look like, to seem like, one thinks that + S + V

주로 mainly

간식 snack

사 주다 to buy someone something

따로 separately, individually, particularly

전화 phone call

연락을 하다 to contact, to call

식사 meal

약속을 잡다 to make an appointment, to arrange a meeting

관심을 보이다 to show interest

A : 마음에 드는 사람이 생기면 먼저 다가가는 편이에요?

If you find someone you like, do you tend to approach them first?

B : 아니요. 저는 마음에 드는 사람 앞에서는 아무 말도 못해요.

No. In front of someone I like, I can't say anything.

A : 그럼 어떻게 상대방에게 표현해요?

Then how do you express your feelings to the other person?

B : 그래서 저는 주로 짝사랑만 해요.

That's why I usually only have crushes.

Vocabulary Review

생기다 to happen, to be formed, to be made

-(으)ㄴ/는 편이다 to tend to; would usually + V

앞 front

말 word, language, speech

상대방 the other person/party

표현하다 to express

주로 mainly

짝사랑 unrequited love, crush

-만 only

연애를 할 때 결혼을 염두에 두고 만나는 편이에요?

When you date someone, do you usually see him/her with marriage in mind?

Similar Questions

연애를 할 때 결혼을 생각하며 만나는 편이에요?

When you date someone, do you usually date him/her with marriage in mind?

연애를 할 때 항상 결혼을 생각하는 편이에요?

Do you tend to always think of marriage when you date someone?

연애를 할 때 결혼에 대해 생각하는 편이에요?

When you date someone, do you tend to think about marriage?

Key Grammar Point

-을/를 염두에 두다

Noun + -을/를 염두에 두다 = to bear + Noun + in mind

Ex) 목표 + -를 염두에 두다

⇨ 목표를 염두에 두다 = **to bear the goal in mind**

네. 저는 연애를 할 때 결혼을 염두에 두고 만나는 편이에요.

Yes. When I date someone, I usually have marriage in mind.

More Answers

네. 저는 연애를 할 때 결혼을 생각하며 만나는 편이에요.

Yes. When I date someone, I tend to date him/her with marriage in mind.

아니요. 저는 연애를 할 때 결혼에 대해 전혀 생각하지 않아요.

No. When I date someone, I don't think about marriage at all.

아니요. 저는 연애를 할 때 결혼에 대해 별로 생각하지 않는 편이에요.

No. When I date someone, I usually don'ㄹt think much about marriage.

Vocabulary Review

연애를 하다 to date, to go out with

만나다 to meet

항상 always

전혀 not at all

별로 not really, not particularly

염두에 두다 to consider, to have something in mind

-(으)ㄴ/는 편이다 to tend to; would usually + V

결혼 marriage

생각하다 to think

-에 대해(서) about

연애를 할 때 결혼을 염두에 두고 만나는 편이에요?

Kyeong-eun's Answer

20대 때에는 결혼을 염두에 두고 만나지는 않았어요. 그런데 30대가 되면서는 결혼을 염두에 두고 만났던 거 같아요.

In my 20s, I did not date with marriage in mind. But once I entered my 30s, I think I've started to date people with more consideration toward marriage.

Study Notes

20대 one's twenties

결혼 marriage

염두에 두다 to consider, to have something in mind

만나다 to meet

30대 one's thirties

되다 to become

-(으)ㄴ 것 같다 to look like, to seem like, one thinks that + S + V

A : 연애를 할 때 결혼에 대해 생각하는 편이에요?

When you date someone, do you tend to think about marriage?

B : 네. 저는 사귈 때마다 결혼에 대해 생각해요.

Yes. Whenever I date someone, I think about marriage.

A : 그럼 사귀기 전에 굉장히 신중하겠네요?

Then, aren't you cautious before you date someone?

B : 아니요. 그렇지는 않아요.

No. Not really.

Vocabulary Review

연애 dating, going out with someone

생각하다 to think

사귀다 to date, to go out with

전 before

굉장히 very, extremely

신중하다 to be cautious

그렇다 to be so

-(으)ㄴ/는 편이다 to tend to; would usually + V

-때마다 whenever something happens

결혼 marriage

그럼 then, in that case

연애를 할 때 주로 어떤 문제로 갈등이 생기는 편이에요?

When you date someone, what kind of problems mainly cause trouble?

Similar Questions

연애를 할 때 주로 어떤 면에서 갈등이 생기는 편이에요?

When you date someone, what aspects do you mainly have trouble with?

연애를 할 때 주로 어떤 것 때문에 갈등이 생기는 편이에요?

When you date someone, because of what main reasons do you have trouble with?

연애를 할 때 주로 무엇 때문에 갈등이 생기는 편이에요?

When you date someone, what is the main thing that causes problems?

Key Grammar Point

때문에

Noun + 때문에 = because of + Noun

Ex) 감기 때문에 = **because of a cold**

저는 연애를 할 때 (돈) 문제로 갈등이 생기는 경우가 많아요.

When I date someone, I often have trouble because of (money) problems.

More Answers

저는 연애를 할 때 (종교) 문제로 싸우는 경우가 많아요.

When I date someone, I often fight because of (religion).

저는 연애를 할 때 (성격 차이) 때문에 갈등이 생기는 경우가 많아요.

When I date someone, I often have trouble because of (personality differences).

저는 연애를 할 때 (술) 때문에 싸우는 경우가 많아요.

When I date someone, I often fight because of (alcohol).

Vocabulary Review

주로 mainly

갈등 conflict

돈 money

종교 religion

성격 character, personality

때문에 because of

생기다 to happen, to be formed, to be made

-(으)ㄴ/는 편이다 to tend to; would usually + V

연애를 하다 to date, to go out with

문제 problem

면 side

경우 case

싸우다 to fight

차이 difference

술 alcohol

연애를 할 때 주로 어떤 문제로 갈등이 생기는 편이에요?

Jooyeon's Answer

그건 정말 연애 대상에 따라 달라요. 세상엔 정말 다양한 사람들이 있으니까요. 하지만 대부분의 갈등은 근본적으로 가치관의 차이에서 생기는 것 같아요.

It really depends on who I date. There are really a wide variety of people in the world. However, I think the most trouble is essentially formed from differences in values.

Study Notes

정말 really

세상 world

사람들 people

하지만 but, however

갈등 conflict

가치관 values

차이 difference

대상 object, subject, target

생기다 to happen; to be formed, to be made

-에 따라 다르다 to depend on, to vary depending on

연애 dating, going out with someone

다양하다 to be various, to be diverse

-(으)니까 since (the reason)

대부분 mostly, majority, in the most part

근본적으로 basically, fundamentally

A : 어제 데이트 잘 했어요?

Did your date go well yesterday?

B : 어제 크게 싸우고 헤어질 뻔했어요.

We had a big fight yesterday and we almost broke up.

A : 왜요? 주로 무엇 때문에 갈등이 생기는 편이에요?

Why? For what reason do you normally have problems?

B : 술이죠. 그제 술 마시고 제가 전화를 못 받았거든요.

Alcohol. The day before yesterday, I was drinking and couldn't answer her phone call.

Vocabulary Review

어제 yesterday

-(으)ㄹ 뻔 하다 to almost + V

때문에 because

술 alcohol

전화 phone call

크게 greatly, largely, highly, loudly

헤어지다 to break up (with someone), to part from someone

생기다 to happen, to be formed, to be made

싸우다 to fight

주로 mainly

갈등 conflict

마시다 to drink

받다 to get, to receive

소개팅이나 미팅을 많이 하는 편이에요/편이었어요?

Do you tend to, or did you use to, go on a lot of blind dates or group blind dates?

Similar Questions

소개팅이나 미팅에 많이 나가는 편이에요/편이었어요?

Do you tend to, or did you use to, go on a lot of blind dates or group blind dates?

소개팅이나 미팅에 자주 나가는 편이에요/편이었어요?

Do you tend to, or did you use to, often go on blind dates or group blind dates?

소개팅 주선을 많이 받는 편이에요/편이었어요?

Do you, or did you often, receive requests to go on a blind date?

Key Grammar Point

-(이)나

Noun + -(이)나 = Noun + or

Ex) 아이스크림이나 커피 = ice cream or coffee

네. 소개팅이나 미팅을 많이 하는 편이에요.

Yes. I tend to go on a lot of blind dates or group blind dates.

More Answers

네. 소개팅이나 미팅에 자주 나가는 편이에요/편이었어요.

Yes. I tend to/used to go on a lot of blind dates and group blind dates.

아니요. 소개팅이나 미팅은 많이 안 하는 편이에요/편이었어요.

No. I don't tend to/didn't go on a lot of blind dates or group blind dates.

아니요. 소개팅이나 미팅을 안 좋아하는 편이에요/편이었어요.

No. I usually don't/didn't like blind dates or group blind dates.

Vocabulary Review

소개팅 blind date   미팅 blind date with a group of people

많이 a lot   하다 to do

-(으)ㄴ/는 편이다 to tend to; would usually + V

나가다 to go to (a gathering), to attend (a group meeting)

자주 often

주선 arrangement

받다 to get, to receive

좋아하다 to like

소개팅이나 미팅을 많이 하는 편이에요? 혹은 편이었어요?

Hyeonjeong's Answer

안 하는 편이에요. 왠지 소개팅에 나오는 남자는 별로일 거라는 선입관이 있어요. 그래서 소개팅이 별로 하고 싶지 않아요.

I tend not to. Somehow I have this prejudice that men who go on blind dates won't be that attractive. So, I don't really want to go on blind dates.

Study Notes

왠지 somehow, for some reason

소개팅 blind date

나오다 to come out, to appear; to be released

남자 man, guy

별로 not really, not particularly

선입관 prejudice, stereotype

-고 싶다 to want to + V

A : 소개팅이나 미팅에 많이 나가는 편이에요?

Do you tend to go on a lot of blind dates or group blind dates?

B : 아니요. 근데 미팅은 한 번도 안 해 봐서, 해 보고 싶어요.

No. But I have never gone on a group blind date, so I would like to try.

A : 저도 미팅 재밌을 거 같아요.

I think a group blind date would be fun, too.

B : 제가 친구들 모아 볼게요.

I will see if I can gather some friends.

Vocabulary Review

미팅 blind date with a group of people

많이 a lot

나가다 to go to (a gathering), to attend (a group meeting)

-(으)ㄴ/는 편이다 to tend to; would usually + V

한 번도 not even once

재미있다 to be interesting

친구들 friends

모으다 to collect, to gather, to save

-아/어/여 보다 to try + -ing

내가 좋아하는 사람과 연애를 하는 편이에요, 아니면 나를 좋아하는 사람과 연애를 하는 편이에요?

Do you usually date someone who you like, or someone who likes you?

Similar Questions

본인이 좋아하는 사람과 연애를 하는 편이에요, 아니면 본인을 좋아하는 사람과 연애를 하는 편이에요?

Do you usually date someone who you like or someone who likes you?

본인이 좋아하는 사람과 사귀는 편이에요, 아니면 본인을 좋아하는 사람과 사귀는 편이에요?

Do you usually go out with someone who you like or someone who likes you?

내가 좋아하는 사람과 사귀는 편이에요, 아니면 나를 좋아하는 사람과 사귀는 편이에요?

Do you usually date someone who you like or someone who likes you?

Key Grammar Point

아니면

Noun + 아니면 = Noun + or/if not

Ex) 아이스크림 아니면 커피 = ice cream or coffee

제가 좋아하는 사람과 주로 사귀는 편이에요.

I usually date someone that I like (rather than someone who likes me more).

More Answers

저를 좋아하는 사람과 주로 사귀는 편이에요.

I mainly date people who like me more.

저는 제가 좋아하는 사람하고만 사귀어요.

I only date people who I like more.

저는 저를 좋아하는 사람하고만 사귀어요.

I only date people who like me more.

Vocabulary Review

좋아하다 to like

사람 person

연애를 하다 to date, to go out with

본인 oneself, the said person

사귀다 to date, to go out with

주로 mainly

-만 only

내가 좋아하는 사람과 연애를 하는 편이에요, 아니면 나를
좋아하는 사람과 연애를 하는 편이에요?

Kyung-hwa's Answer

어릴 때는 제가 좋아하는 사람에게만 관심을
가졌었어요. 그런데 지금은 저를 좋아하고,
그것을 적극적으로 표현하는 사람에게 매력
을 느끼는 것 같아요.

When I was younger, I only had interest in people
who I liked. But now, I think I only feel attracted
to people who like me and actively show their
feelings toward me.

Study Notes

어리다 to be young

때 the time, the moment

-만 only

관심 interest

가지다 to have, to possess

적극적으로 actively; aggressively

표현하다 to express

매력 attraction

느끼다 to feel

-(으)ㄴ 것 같다 to look like, to seem like, one thinks that + S + V

A : 전 왜 이렇게 연애를 못 할까요?

Why can't I date anyone?

B : 지은 씨가 좋아하는 사람만 만나려고 하니까 그러는 거예요.

Ji-eun, I think it's because you only want to date someone you like.

A : 그럼 현우 씨는 본인이 좋아하는 사람과 사귀는 편이에요, 아니면 본인을 좋아하는 사람과 사귀는 편이에요?

Then, Hyunwoo, do you usually date someone you like, or someone who likes you?

B : 저는 저를 좋아하는 사람과 연애를 하는 편이죠.

Of course I tend to date someone who likes me.

Vocabulary Review

이렇게 like this

연애 dating, going out with someone

만나다 to meet

-(으)려고 in order to

그렇다 to be so

본인 oneself

-(으)ㄴ/는 편이다 to tend to; would usually + V

My Answers

Write your responses to the following questions below.

Q. 마음에 드는 사람에게 먼저 다가가는 편이에요?

Q. 연애를 할 때 결혼을 염두에 두고 만나는 편이에요?

Q. 연애를 할 때 주로 어떤 문제로 갈등이 생기는 편이에요?

Q. 소개팅이나 미팅을 많이 하는 편이에요/ 편이었어요?

Q. 내가 좋아하는 사람과 연애를 하는 편이에요, 아니 면 나를 좋아하는 사람과 연애를 하는 편이에요?

7.
CELEBRITIES

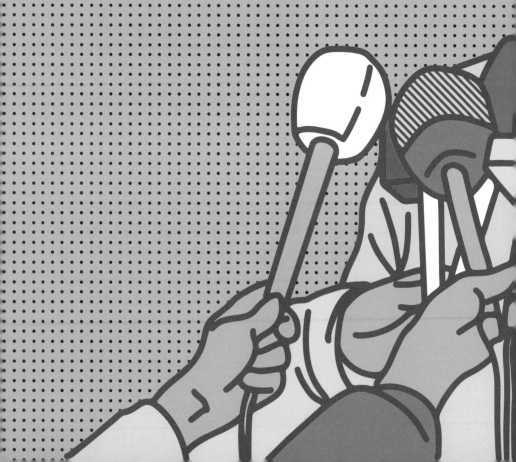

팬클럽에 가입해 본 적 있어요?

Have you ever joined a fan club?

Similar Questions

누구 팬클럽에 가입해 본 적 있어요?

Have you ever joined a fan club for someone?

팬클럽으로 활동해 본 적 있어요?

Have you ever done any fan club activities?

팬클럽에 가입해서 활동해 본 적 있어요?

Have you ever joined a fan club and done any activities?

Key Grammar Point

-(으)로

Noun + -(으)로 = as + Noun

Ex) 회원으로 = as a member

네. (H.O.T.) 팬클럽에 가입했었어요.

Yes. I joined the (H.O.T.) fan club.

More Answers

네. (G.O.D.) 팬클럽으로 활동했었어요.
Yes. I was a member of the (G.O.D.) fan club.

아니요. 연예인 팬클럽에 가입해 본 적은 없어요.
No. I have never joined a celebrity fan club.

아니요. 한 번도 팬클럽에 가입해 본 적은 없어요.
No. I have never joined a fan club.

Vocabulary Review

팬클럽 fan club

가입하다 to join

-(으)ㄴ 적(이) 있다 to have + V-ed (experience)

누구 who

활동하다 to work (as), to be active in a certain field

연예인 celebrity, entertainer

한 번도 not even once

팬클럽에 가입해 본 적 있어요?

Kyung-hwa's Answer

팬클럽에 가입해 본 적은 딱 한 번 있어요. 중학교 때 Backstreet Boys 팬클럽에 가입했었어요.

I've joined a fan club just once. When I was in middle school, I joined the Backstreet Boys fan club.

Study Notes

가입하다 to join

딱 just, exactly

한 번 once

중학교 middle school

A : 팬클럽에 가입해서 활동해 본 적 있어요?

Have you ever joined and became a member of a fan club?

B : 저 이번에 EXO 팬클럽에 가입했어요.
이 티셔츠 보세요.

I recently joined the EXO fan club. Look at this t-shirt.

A : 오! 이거 EXO 팬클럽만 살 수 있는 티셔츠
맞죠?

Wow. This is a t-shirt that only EXO fan club members can buy, right?

B : 네, 맞아요.

Yes, that's right.

Vocabulary Review

가입하다 to join

이번에 this time

보다 to see, to watch

이거 this one

사다 to buy

-(으)ㄹ 수 있다 to be able to + V

맞다 to fit, to match, to be right

-(으)ㄴ 적(이) 있다 to have + V-ed (experience)

활동하다 to work, to act

티셔츠 t-shirt

개인적으로 친한 연예인/유명인이 있어요?

Is there a celebrity with whom you are personally close?

Similar Questions

개인적으로 친분이 있는 연예인/유명인이 있어요?

Is there a celebrity with whom you are acquainted?

개인적으로 알고 지내는 연예인/유명인이 있어요?

Is there a celebrity who you know personally?

개인적으로 친하게 지내는 연예인/유명인이 있어요?

Is there a celebrity who you know well personally?

Key Grammar Point

개인적으로

개인 = **individual** / -적 = **modifier** / -으로 = **adverb particle**
⇨ 개인적으로 = **personally, individually**

Ex) 개인적으로 알다 = **to know in person**

네. (송중기)(이)랑 친한 사이예요.

Yes. I am close friends with (Song Joong-ki).

More Answers

네. (보아)(이)랑 예전부터 아는 사이예요.

Yes. I've known (BoA) for a long time now.

아니요. 친하게 지내는 연예인/유명인은 없어요.

No. There is no celebrity who I am close with.

아니요. 개인적으로 친분이 있는 연예인/유명인은 없어요.

No. There is no celebrity with whom I am personally close.

Vocabulary Review

개인적으로 personally

유명인 celebrity

알다 to know

친하다 to be close with, to be close friends with

알고 지내다 to keep up an acquaintance with

친하게 지내다 to be on intimate terms with

예전부터 from old times, from a long time ago

연예인 celebrity, entertainer

친분이 있다 to be acquainted

사이 relationship

개인적으로 친한 연예인/유명인이 있어요?

Seokjin's Answer

네. 있어요. 원래 직업이 연예인은 아닌데 우연히 나간 어느 방송 때문에 아주 유명해진 친구가 있어요. 이름을 대면 아마 누구든지 알 거예요.

Yes, there is. He is not a celebrity because of his job, but I have a friend who became famous because of a TV show that he was on by accident. I think everyone will know if I say his name.

Study Notes

원래 original, existing

우연히 by accident

방송 broadcasting

아주 very, extremely

유명하다 to be famous

친구 friend

이름을 대다 to mention someone's name

아마 probably, perhaps

누구든지 anybody

알다 to know

직업 job

나가다 to go on (a TV show)

때문에 because of

A : 개인적으로 친하게 지내는 연예인이나 유명인이 있어요?

Is there a celebrity you are personally close with?

B : 네, 있어요.

Yes, there is.

A : 누구요? 저 만나게 해 주세요.

Who? Let me meet him/her.

B : 아, 그렇게 유명한 사람은 아니에요.

Oh, it's not someone that famous.

Vocabulary Review

개인적으로 personally

친하게 지내다 to be on intimate terms with

연예인 celebrity, entertainer

유명인 celebrity, famous person

만나다 to meet

그렇게 so, like that

유명하다 to be famous

연예인/유명인이 되고 싶다고 생각했던 적 있어요?

Have you ever thought you wanted to become a celebrity?

Similar Questions

연예인/유명인이 되고 싶다고 생각해 본 적 있어요?

Have you ever thought you wanted to become a celebrity?

연예인/유명인을 꿈꿔 본 적 있어요?

Have you ever dreamed of becoming a celebrity?

연예인/유명인을 꿈꿨던 적 있어요?

Have you ever dreamed of becoming a famous person?

Key Grammar Point

-(ㄴ)다고 생각하다

Verb stem + -(ㄴ)다고 = to think that + S + V-적 = modifier

Ex) 좋다고 생각해요. = I think it's good.

네. 어렸을 때 (대통령)이/가 꿈이었어요.

Yes. When I was younger, my dream was to become (the President).

More Answers

네. 지금도 (영화배우)이/가 되고 싶어요.
Yes. I still want to be (a movie actor/actress).

아니요. 연예인/유명인이 되고 싶다고 생각했던 적은 없어요.
No. I have never thought I wanted to become a celebrity.

아니요. 연예인/유명인이 되고 싶었던 적은 없어요.
No. I have never wanted to become a famous person.

Vocabulary Review

연예인 celebrity, entertainer

-고 싶다 to want to + V

되다 to become

어리다 to be young

대통령 president

꿈 dream

영화배우 movie actor/actress

-(으)ㄴ 적(이) 있다 to have + V-ed (experience)

유명인 celebrity, famous person

생각하다 to think

꿈꾸다 to dream

연예인/유명인이 되고 싶다고 생각했던 적 있어요?

Jooyeon's Answer

아니요. 유명한 사람이 되고 싶었던 적은 없어요. 주목 받는 것을 그렇게 좋아하지 않아서 그런 것 같아요.

No. I have never wanted to become a famous person. I think it's because I do not like receiving attention.

Study Notes

유명하다 to be famous

사람 person

되다 to become

-고 싶다 to want to + V

주목 받다 to get attention

좋아하다 to like

그렇다 to be so

-(으)ㄴ 것 같다 to look like, to seem like, one thinks that + S + V

A : 연예인을 꿈꿔 본 적 있어요?
Have you ever dreamed of becoming a celebrity?

B : 사실은 지금도 연예인이 되고 싶어요.
Actually, I still want to become a celebrity.

A : 정말요? 어떤 분야요?
Really? In which area?

B : 배우가 되는 게 꿈이에요.
My dream is to become an actor.

Vocabulary Review

연예인 celebrity, entertainer

사실은 actually

되다 to become

정말 really

어떤 which

분야 field

배우 actor, actress

꿈 dream

-(으)ㄴ 적(이) 있다 to have + V-ed (experience)

꿈꾸다 to dream

지금도 even now

-고 싶다 to want to + V

태어나서 처음으로 실물을 본 연예인/유명인은 누구였어요?

Who was the first celebrity you've seen in person?

Similar Questions

태어나서 처음으로 본 연예인/유명인은 누구였어요?
Who was the first celebrity that you've seen in your life?

태어나서 실제로 처음 본 연예인/유명인은 누구였어요?
Who was the first celebrity in your life that you've seen in person?

처음 실물로 본 연예인/유명인은 누구였어요?
Which celebrity have you seen in person for the first time?

Key Grammar Point

태어나서 처음으로

태어나다 = to be born
-아/어/여서 = after
처음으로 = as the first
⇨ 태어나서 처음으로 = for the first time in one's life

태어나서 처음으로 실물을 본 연예인/유명인은 (정우성)이었어요/였어요.

The first celebrity that I've seen in my life was (Jeong Woo-seong).

More Answers

태어나서 처음 실제로 본 연예인/유명인은 (김희선)이에요/예요.
The first celebrity I've seen in my life was (Kim Hee-seon).

(이효리)이/가 제가 태어나서 실제로 처음 본 연예인/유명인이었어요.
(Lee Hyori) was the first celebrity that I've seen in my life.

(박명수)이/가 실물로 처음 본 연예인/유명인이었어요.
(Park Myeong-soo) was the first celebrity I've seen in person.

Vocabulary Review

태어나다 to be born
처음으로 for the first time
실물 the real thing
보다 to watch, to see
누구 who
실제로 actually, in reality
처음 first

태어나서 처음으로 실물을 본 연예인/유명인은 누구였어요?

Hyeonjeong's Answer

스쳐 지나가면서는 여러 명 봤는데, 오랜 시간 본 사람은 박명수요. 저녁을 먹으러 갔는데 맞은편 테이블에 앉아서 밥을 먹고 있었어요.

I've seen many just passing by, but the one person I've seen for longer than just a few seconds is Park Myeong-soo. I went to have dinner, and he was eating at the table across from me.

Study Notes

스쳐 지나가다 to pass someone by

보다 to see, to watch

시간 time

저녁 dinner

-(으)러 가다 to go + V-ing

맞은편 opposite side

앉다 to sit

밥 meal, food, rice

먹다 to eat

-고 있다 to be V-ing

여러 명 several people

오랜 long, a while

사람 person

먹다 to eat

A : 연예인 실제로 본 적 있어요?

Have you ever seen a celebrity in real life?

B : 네. 몇 명 있어요.

Yes. A few.

A : 태어나서 처음으로 본 연예인은 누구였어요?

Who was the first celebrity you've ever seen?

B : 음... 잘 기억이 안 나요.

Hmm... I can't remember.

Vocabulary Review

실제로 actually, in reality

보다 to see, to watch

태어나다 to be born

처음 first

기억이 나다 to remember

실제로 만나서 이야기해 보고 싶은 연예인/유명인이 있어요?

Is there a celebrity who you would want to meet and talk to in person?

Similar Questions

실제로 만나서 이야기해 보고 싶은 연예인/유명인이 있다면 누구예요?

If there is a celebrity who you would like to actually meet and talk to, who would it be?

실제로 만나 보고 싶은 연예인/유명인이 있어요?

Is there a celebrity who you would like to meet in person?

실제로 만나 보고 싶은 연예인/유명인이 있다면 누구예요?

If there is a celebrity who you would like to meet in person, who would it be?

Key Grammar Point

실제로

실제로 + Verb = Verb + in person/reality

Ex) 실제로 봤어요. = I saw it in person.

네. 저는 (성룡)(이)랑 실제로 만나서 이야기해 보고 싶어요.

Yes. I would like to meet (Jackie Chan) in person and talk with him.

More Answers

네. 저는 (브래드 피트)을/를 실제로 만나 보고 싶어요.
Yes. I want to meet (Brad Pitt) in person.

아니요. 실제로 만나 보고 싶은 연예인/유명인은 없어요.
No. There is no celebrity that I would like to meet in person.

아니요. 저는 만나 보고 싶은 연예인/유명인이 없어요.
No. There is no celebrity that I want to meet.

Vocabulary Review

실제로 actually, in reality
만나다 to meet
이야기하다 to talk
-고 싶다 to want to + V

> # 실제로 만나서 이야기해 보고 싶은 연예인/유명인이 있어요?

Kyeong-eun's Answer

네. 저는 유재석을 실제로 만나서 이야기해 보고 싶어요. 배울 점이 정말 많을 거 같아요.

Yes. I want to meet Yoo Jae-seok and talk with him in person. I think I would learn a lot of things from him.

Study Notes

실제로 actually, in reality

만나다 to meet

이야기하다 to talk

-아/어/여 보다 to try + V-ing

-고 싶다 to want to + V

배우다 to learn

-(으)ㄴ 점 thing, aspect

정말 really

많다 to be a lot

A : 실제로 만나 보고 싶은 연예인이 있어요?

Is there a celebrity who you would want to meet in real life?

B : 소녀시대요.

Girls' Generation.

A : 아, 소녀시대! 저도 소녀시대 실제로 만나 보고 싶네요.

Oh, Girls' Generation. I also want to meet Girls' Generation in real life.

B : 실제로 만나면 떨려서 아무 말도 못할 거 같아요.

If I actually met them, I would be too nervous to say anything.

Vocabulary Review

실제로 actually, in reality

만나다 to meet

-고 싶다 to want to + V

연예인 celebrity, entertainer

떨리다 to shake, to vibrate, to tremble

말 word, language, speech

My Answers

Write your responses to the following questions below.

Q. 팬클럽에 가입해 본 적 있어요?

Q. 개인적으로 친한 연예인/유명인이 있어요?

Q. 연예인/유명인이 되고 싶다고 생각 했던 적 있어요?

Q. 태어나서 처음으로 실물을 본 연예 인/유명인은 누구였어요?

Q. 실제로 만나서 이야기해 보고 싶은 연예인/유명인이 있어요?

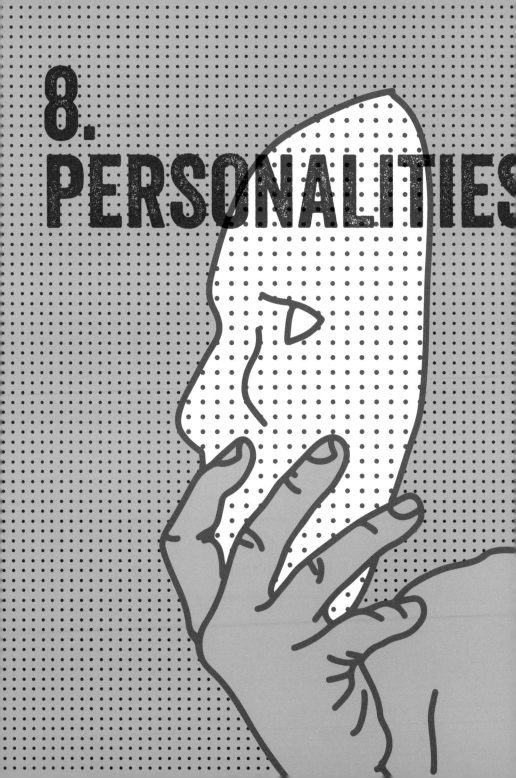

8.
PERSONALITIES

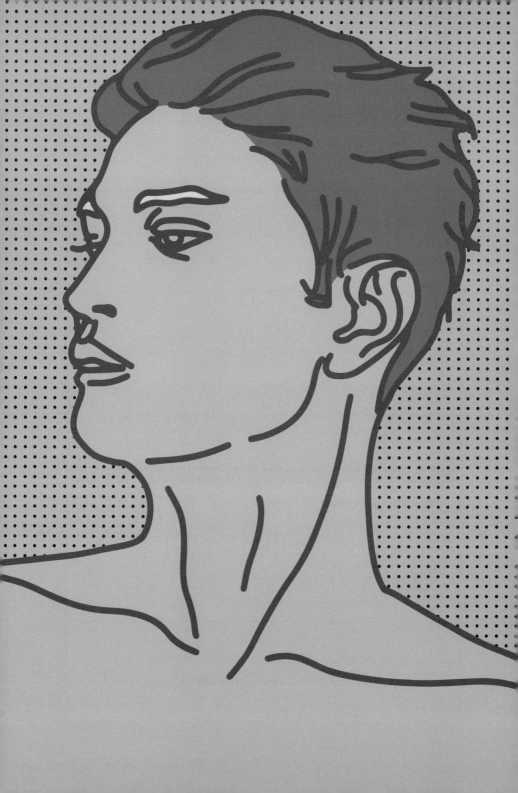

성격은 바뀔 수 있다고 믿어요?

Do you believe that someone's personality can change?

Similar Questions

성격은 바뀔 수 있다고 생각해요?

Do you think personalities can change?

성격은 바뀔 수 있는 거라고 믿어요?

Do you believe that personalities are something that can change?

성격은 바뀔 수 있는 거라고 생각해요?

Do you think that personalities are something that can change?

Key Grammar Point

-(ㄴ/는)(다)고 믿다

Verb stem + -(ㄴ/는)(다)고 믿다 = to believe that + S + V

Ex) 도움이 되다 + -(ㄴ/는)(다)고 믿다

⇨ 도움이 된다고 믿어요. **(I believe it is helpful.)**

네. 성격은 바뀔 수 있다고 믿어요.

Yes. I believe personalities can change.

More Answers

네. 성격은 바뀔 수 있다고 생각해요.
Yes. I believe personalities can change.

아니요. 성격은 바뀔 수 없는 거라고 생각해요.
No. I think personalities are something that can't change.

아니요. 성격은 바뀌지 않는다고 생각해요.
No. I think personalities don't change.

Vocabulary Review

성격 character, personality
바뀌다 to be changed
믿다 to believe, to trust
생각하다 to think

성격은 바뀔 수 있다고 믿어요?

Kyung-hwa's Answer

네. 저는 바뀔 수 있다고 믿어요. 특히나 충격적인 사건을 겪거나 큰 깨달음을 얻었을 때 성격이 변하는 것 같아요.

Yes. I believe they can change. I think a person's personality changes especially after he/she has experienced a shocking incident or has realized something important.

Study Notes

바뀌다 to be changed

믿다 to believe

충격적이다 to be shocking

겪다 to experience; to undertake, to undergo

큰 big

깨달음 enlightenment

얻다 to get, to gain, to obtain

성격 character, personality

변하다 to be changed

-(으)ㄴ 것 같다 to look like, to seem like, one thinks that + S + V

-(으)ㄹ 수 있다 to be able to + V

특히(나) especially, particularly

사건 case, event, incident

Sample Dialogue

A : 남자 친구랑 잘 지내요?

Is everything going well with your boyfriend?

B : 아니요. 요즘 맨날 싸워요. 서로 성격이 너무 달라요. 민수 씨는 사람 성격이 바뀔 수 있다고 생각해요?

No. These days we fight every day. Our personalities are so different from one another. Min-soo, do you think a person's personality can change?

A : 아니요. 저는 사람 성격은 쉽게 바뀌지 않는다고 생각해요. 그냥 다르다는 걸 인정해 봐요.

No. I think a person's personality doesn't change easily. Just try accepting that you guys are different from each other.

B : 네. 근데 그게 너무 어려워요.

Yeah, but it's really difficult.

Vocabulary Review

남자 친구 boyfriend

요즘 these days

싸우다 to fight

성격 character, personality

다르다 to be different

바뀌다 to be changed

인정하다 to acknowledge, to admit

어렵다 to be difficult, to be hard

잘 지내다 to get along with

맨날 always, daily, every day

서로 each other

너무 so, really; too much

사람 person

생각하다 to think

쉽게 easily

성격이 좋다는 이야기를 많이 듣는 편이에요?

Do you often hear that you have a good personality?

Similar Questions

사람들한테 성격이 좋다는 이야기를 많이 듣는 편이에요?

Do you often hear from people that you have a good personality?

사람들한테 성격이 좋다는 칭찬을 많이 듣는 편이에요?

Do you get compliments from people that you have a good personality?

성격이 좋다는 이야기를 자주 들어요?

Are you often told that you have a good personality?

Key Grammar Point

-(ㄴ/는)다는 이야기

Verb stem + -(ㄴ/는)다는 이야기
= a story that says + S + V / people saying that S + V

Ex) 키가 크다 + -(ㄴ/는)다는 이야기
⇨ 키가 크다는 이야기 = **(people) saying that (someone) is tall**

네. 성격이 좋다는 이야기를 많이 듣는 편이에요.

Yes. I tend to hear a lot of people say that I have a good personality.

More Answers

네. 사람들한테 성격이 좋다는 이야기를 많이 듣는 편이에요.

Yes. I tend to hear a lot of people say that I have a good personality.

아니요. 성격 좋다는 이야기는 별로 못 들어 봤어요.

No. I haven't heard a lot of people say that I have a good personality.

아니요. 성격 좋다는 칭찬은 별로 못 들어 봤어요.

No. I haven't heard a lot of compliments about having a good personality.

Vocabulary Review

성격 character, personality

이야기 story, chat

듣다 to listen

칭찬 compliment

자주 often

많이 a lot

별로 not really, not particularly

좋다 to be good, to like

많이 a lot

사람들 people

성격이 좋다는 이야기를 많이 듣는 편이에요?

Seokjin's Answer

어렸을 때는 많이 들었었는데, 20대가 된 후로 잘 못 듣고 있어요. 이기적인 성격이라는 얘기를 가끔 들을 때가 있는데, 그때마다 반성하고 있어요.

I did when I was younger, but not so much after I entered my 20s. I hear people say that I have a selfish personality, and whenever I hear that, I reflect on myself.

Study Notes

어리다 to be young

많이 a lot

20대 one's twenties

이기적이다 to be selfish

성격 character, personality

얘기 story, word

가끔 sometimes

그때마다 on all such occasions, whenever that happens

반성하다 to regret, to reflect

때 the time, the moment

듣다 to listen

후 after

A : 민주 씨는 성격이 좋다는 이야기 자주 들어요?

Min-joo, do you often hear people say you have a good personality?

B : 저요? 아니요.

Me? No.

A : 진짜요? 그런 말 많이 들을 거 같은데.

Really? You seem like you would hear that often.

B : 아니에요. 오히려 차가워 보인다는 말을 많이 들어요.

No. On the contrary, I often hear that I seem cold.

Vocabulary Review

성격 character, personality

이야기 story, chat

듣다 to listen

그런 such

많이 a lot

오히려 rather, on the contrary

보이다 to be seen, to seem, to show

좋다 to be good, to like

자주 often

진짜 really, very, so

말 word, language, speech

듣다 to listen

차갑다 to be cold

-(으)ㄴ 것 같다 to look like, to seem like; one thinks that + S + V

부모님 두 분 중에 어느 쪽 성격을 더 닮았어요?

Between your parents, whose personality do you take after more?

Similar Questions

부모님 두 분 중에 어느 분의 성격을 더 닮았어요?

Between your parents, which person's personality do you take after more?

어머니 아버지 중에 어느 쪽 성격을 더 닮았어요?

Between your mother and your father, whose personality do you take after more?

어머니 아버지 중에 어느 분의 성격을 더 닮았어요?

Between your mother and your father, which person's personality do you take after more?

Key Grammar Point

어느

어느 + Noun = which + Noun

Ex) 어느 집이에요? = **Which house is it?**

저는 (엄마) 성격을 더 닮았어요.

I take after (my mother)'s personality more.

More Answers

제 성격은 (아빠) 성격이랑 비슷해요.
My personality is similar to my (father)'s personality.

저는 부모님 성격을 별로 안 닮았어요.
I don't take after my parents' personalities that much.

저는 부모님 성격을 전혀 안 닮았어요.
I don't take after my parents' personalities at all.

Vocabulary Review

부모님 parents

어느 쪽 which side

닮다 to resemble, to look like

엄마 mom, mother

아빠 dad, father

별로 not really, not particularly

전혀 not at all

분 person (honorific)

성격 character, personality

부모님 두 분 중에 어느 쪽 성격을 더 닮았어요?

Jooyeon's Answer

두 분의 성격을 모두 골고루 가지고 있는 것 같아요. 그런데 엄마는 항상 제가 아빠랑 성격이 똑같다고 말씀하세요. 장난치는 것을 좋아하고 또 고민이 많은 점이 아빠와 많이 닮은 것 같아요.

I think I have both of their personalities equally. But my mom always says that I have the same personality as my father. I think I am similar to my father in that I like joking around and I often have a lot on my mind.

Study Notes

분 counter for people (honorific)

모두 all, everything

가지다 to have, to possess

항상 always

똑같다 to be same

장난치다 to joke, to make fun of

또 also

많다 to be a lot

닮다 to resemble, to look like

성격 character, personality

골고루 evenly, equally

엄마 mom, mother

아빠 dad, father

말씀하시다 to tell, to say (honorific)

좋아하다 to like

고민 worry, trouble

-(으)ㄴ 점 thing, aspect

A : 수현 씨, 어머니랑 진짜 똑같이 생겼네요?

Soo-hyeon, you really look exactly like your mother!

B : 네. 닮았다는 말 많이 들어요.

Yes, I hear that I look like her quite often.

A : 성격은요? 부모님 두 분 중에 어느 분의 성격을 더 닮았어요?

How about your personality? Between your two parents, whose personality do you take after more?

B : 성격은 아버지 닮았어요.

I take after my father's personality.

Vocabulary Review

어머니 mother

똑같이 same

말 word, language, speech

듣다 to listen

생기다 to happen, to be formed, to be made

부모님 parents

분 counter for people (honorific)

아버지 father

진짜 really, very, so

닮다 to resemble, to look like

많이 a lot

성격 character, personality

자신의 성격이 크게 바뀌었던 시기가 있었어요?

Was there a moment when your personality changed a lot?

Similar Questions

자신의 성격이 크게 바뀌었던 때가 있었어요?
Was there a time when your personality changed a lot?

자신의 성격이 크게 변했던 시기가 있었어요?
Was there a moment when your personality transformed a lot?

자신의 성격이 크게 변했던 때가 있었어요?
Was there a time when your personality transformed a lot?

Key Grammar Point

자신의

자신의 + Noun = one's (own) + Noun

Ex) 자신의 얼굴 = one's own face

네. 저는 (사춘기) 때 성격이 크게 바뀌었어요.

Yes. My personality changed a lot (during puberty).

More Answers

네. 저는 (군대 가)고 나서 성격이 크게 바뀌었어요.

Yes. My personality changed greatly after (starting military service).

아니요. 저는 어렸을 때부터 이런 성격이었어요.

No. I have always had this personality since I was little.

아니요. 저는 어렸을 때부터 지금까지 성격이 똑같아요.

No. From when I was little until now, my personality has been the same.

Vocabulary Review

자신 oneself

크게 greatly, largely, highly, loudly

시기 time, period, moment

변하다 to be changed

군대 military, armed forces

어리다 to be young

이런 such, like this

똑같다 to be the same, to be equal

성격 character, personality

바뀌다 to be changed

때 time, moment

사춘기 puberty, adolescence

-고 나서 after + V-ing

-때부터 since when S + V-ed

-까지 until

자신의 성격이 크게 바뀌었던 시기가 있었어요?

Hyeonjeong's Answer

대학교에 올라가면서 좀 많이 바뀌었던 것 같아요. 한 교실에서 오랜 시간 있다가 대학교에 가면서 교실을 자주 이동하는 생활을 하다 보니 행동 패턴이 달라지고, 그러면서 성격도 좀 달라졌던 거 같아요.

I think my personality changed a lot as I entered college. In high school I was in one classroom for a long time, but in college, I started moving classrooms a lot; therefore my behavioral patterns changed, and in the process, I think my personality also changed a bit.

Study Notes

대학교 university, college

많이 a lot

교실 class

시간 time

이동하다 to move (location)

행동 action, behavior

성격 character, personality

올라가다 to go up, to increase

바뀌다 to be changed

오랜 long

자주 often

생활 life, living

패턴 pattern

좀 a little bit, kind of

-다 보니 while + V-ing for a while one realizes ...

달라지다 to change, to alter, to become different

A : 살면서 성격이 크게 변했던 때가 있었어요?

Was there a time when your personality changed a lot?

B : 저는 사춘기 이후에 변한 거 같아요.

I think my personality changed after puberty.

A : 어떻게요?

How?

B : 사춘기 이후부터 조용한 성격이 되었어요.

I became a quieter person after puberty.

살다 to live

성격 character, personality

크게 greatly, largely, highly, loudly

변하다 to change

때 the time, the moment

사춘기 puberty, adolescence

이후 after

조용하다 to be quiet

되다 to become

Q

자신과 비슷한 성격을 가진 사람들과 주로 어울리는 편이에요?

Do you usually hang out with people who have a similar personality to yours?

Similar Questions

자신과 비슷한 성격을 가진 사람들과 친하게 지내는 편이에요?

Do you tend to be close with people who have a similar personality to yours?

자신과 비슷한 성격을 가진 사람들에게 호감을 느끼는 편이에요?

Do you tend to like people who have a similar personality to yours?

자신과 성격이 비슷한 사람들과 주로 어울리는 편이에요?

Do you tend to mainly hang out with people who have a similar personality to yours?

Key Grammar Point

-에게

Noun + -에게 = to + Noun

Ex) 친구에게 = **to a friend**

네. 저는 저랑 비슷한 성격을 가진 사람들하고 주로 어울리는 편이에요.

Yes. I tend to mainly hang out with people who have a similar personality to mine.

More Answers

네. 저는 저랑 성격이 비슷한 사람들하고 주로 어울리는 편이에요.

Yes. I tend to mainly hang out with people who have similar personalities to mine.

아니요. 저는 오히려 저랑 성격이 반대인 사람들과 친하게 지내는 편이에요.

No. On the contrary, I tend to be close with people whose personalities are the opposite of mine.

아니요. 저는 오히려 저랑 성격이 반대인 친구들이 많은 편이에요.

No. On the contrary, I tend to have a lot of friends whose personalities are the opposite of mine.

Vocabulary Review

자신 oneself

가지다 to have

친하게 지내다 to be on intimate terms with

호감 good feeling, positive feeling

느끼다 to feel

어울리다 to get along with

오히려 rather, on the contrary

반대 the opposite, the reverse

많다 to be a lot

비슷하다 to be similar

사람들 people

자신과 비슷한 성격을 가진 사람들과 주로 어울리는 편이에요?

Kyeong-eun's Answer

어렸을 때는 저와 다른 성격을 가진 사람들과 주로 어울리는 편이었어요. 그런데 이제는 제 성격이 그 사람들 성격과 비슷해진 거 같아요.

When I was younger, I would mainly hang out with people who had personalities that were different from mine. But now, I think my personality has become similar to theirs.

Study Notes

어리다 to be young

다른 different, other

성격 character, personality

사람들 people

주로 mainly

어울리다 to get along with

-(으)ㄴ/는 편이다 to tend to; would usually + V

이제 now, from now on

비슷하다 to be similar

-아/어/여지다 to become + adj.

때 the time, the moment

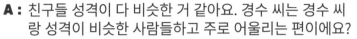

A : 친구들 성격이 다 비슷한 거 같아요. 경수 씨는 경수 씨 랑 성격이 비슷한 사람들하고 주로 어울리는 편이에요?

I think all of your friends have similar personalities. Gyeong-soo, do you tend to mainly hang out with people who have similar personalities to yours?

B : 네. 친구들 성격이 다 비슷비슷해서 너무 편해요.

Yes. My friends all have similar personalities, so it's very comfortable.

A : 저는 저랑 성격이 다른 사람들하고 주로 어울리는 편이 에요.

I tend to mainly hang out with people who have different personalities to mine.

B : 성격이 다 다른 사람들끼리 만나면 재밌긴 할 것 같아요.

I think it would be fun for sure if people with all different kinds of personalities would meet.

Vocabulary Review

친구들 friends

비슷하다 to be similar

주로 mainly

비슷하다 to be similar

편하다 to be comfortable

재밌다 to be interesting

같다 to be same

-끼리 among (oneselves), similar things together

성격 character, personality

사람들 people

어울리다 to get along with

너무 so, really, too much

다르다 to be different

My Answers

Write your responses to the following questions below.

Q. 성격은 바뀔 수 있다고 믿어요?

Q. 성격이 좋다는 이야기를 많이 듣는 편이에요?

Q. 부모님 두 분 중에 어느 쪽 성격을 더 닮았어요?

Q. 자신의 성격이 크게 바뀌었던 시기가 있었어요?

Q. 자신과 비슷한 성격을 가진 사람들과 주로 어울리는 편이에요?

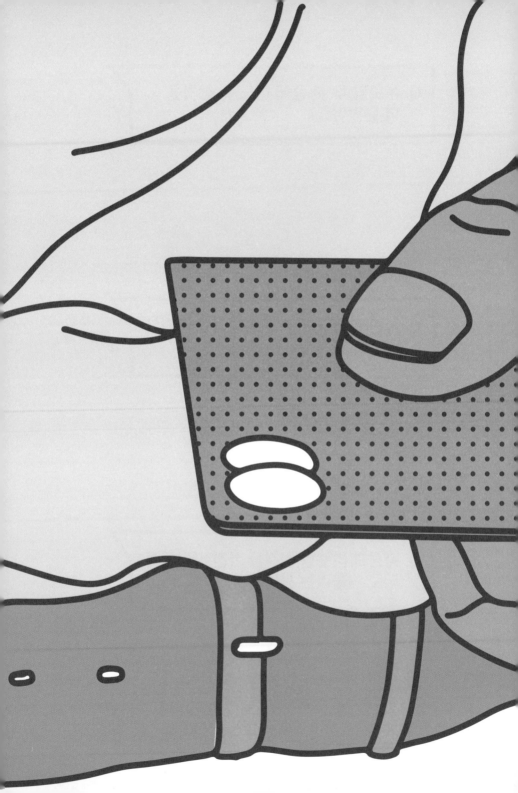

9.
SPENDING
HABITS

어떤 항목에 돈을 가장 많이 써요?

On which item do you spend the most money?

Similar Questions

돈을 가장 많이 쓰는 항목은 뭐예요?
What is the item that you spend the most money on?

가장 지출이 많은 항목은 뭐예요?
Which item do you spend the most money on?

어디에 돈을 가장 많이 써요?
Where do you spend the most amount of money?

Key Grammar Point

가장 많이

가장 = **the most**

많이 = **a lot, in a large amount**

⇨ 가장 많이 = **the most, in the biggest amount**

Ex) 가장 많이 가는 카페 = **the cafe that you go to most often**

저는 (먹는 것)에 돈을 가장 많이 써요.

I spend the most money on (eating).

More Answers

저는 다른 곳보다 (문화생활)에 돈을 가장 많이 써요.
I spend the most money on (cultural activities) more than anything else.

저는 다른 데보다 (술 마시)는 데에 돈을 가장 많이 써요.
More than anything else, I spend the most money on (drinking).

저는 (옷) 사는 데에 돈을 가장 많이 써요.
I spend the most money on buying (clothes).

Vocabulary Review

어떤 which

돈 money

많이 a lot

먹다 to eat

문화생활 cultural life/activities

옷 clothes

항목 item

가장 the most

쓰다 to use, to spend

다른 different, other

술 마시다 to drink (alcohol)

사다 to buy

어떤 항목에 돈을 가장 많이 써요?

Kyung-hwa's Answer

저는 항상 달라지는 것 같은데, 또래 친구들보다 많이 쓰는 항목이라면 문화생활일 것 같아요. 특히 뮤지컬 보는 것을 굉장히 좋아하는데, 티켓값이 워낙 비싸서 자주 보지 않는데도 출혈이 꽤 커요.

I think it always changes for me, but one area where I spend more money than my peers is on cultural activities. I especially like musicals, but the ticket prices are really high, so I can't see them often. But even so, I spend quite a lot on them.

Study Notes

항상 always

-아/어/여지다 to become + adj.

친구들 friends

쓰다 to use

문화생활 cultural life/activities

뮤지컬 musical

굉장히 very, extremely

티켓값 ticket price

비싸다 to be expensive

출혈 bleeding

크다 to be big

다르다 to be different

또래 peer, same age group

많이 a lot

항목 item

특히 especially, particularly

보다 to see, to watch

좋아하다 to like

워낙 so, very, by nature

자주 often

꽤 quite

A : 어디에 돈을 가장 많이 써요?
Where do you spend the most amount of money?

B : 저는 쇼핑하는 데 돈을 가장 많이 써요.
I spend the most amount of money on shopping.

A : 주로 어디에서 쇼핑해요?
Where do you usually do your shopping?

B : 주로 인터넷으로 쇼핑하는 편이에요.
I usually do my shopping on the Internet.

Vocabulary Review

돈 money

가장 the most

많이 a lot

쓰다 to use, to spend

쇼핑하다 to shop, to go shopping

주로 mainly

인터넷 the Internet

-(으)ㄴ/는 편이다 to tend to; would usually + V

언제까지 부모님께 용돈을 받아 생활했어요?

Until when did you live off an allowance from your parents?

Similar Questions

언제까지 부모님한테 용돈을 받아 생활했어요?

Until when did you live off an allowance from your parents?

언제까지 부모님한테 용돈을 받아 썼어요?

Until when did you receive and use an allowance from your parents?

언제까지 부모님한테 용돈을 받았어요?

Until when did you receive an allowance from your parents?

Key Grammar Point

언제까지

언제 = **when** / -까지 = **until** ⇨ 언제까지 = **until when**

Ex) 언제까지 기다려야 돼요? = **Until when do we have to wait?**

저는 (대학교) 때까지 부모님께 용돈을 받아 생활했어요.

I lived off an allowance from my parents until (college).

More Answers

저는 (고등학교) 때까지 부모님한테 용돈을 받아 썼어요.
I lived off an allowance from my parents until (high school).

저는 (스무 살) 때까지 부모님한테 용돈을 받았어요.
I received an allowance from my parents until I was (20 years old).

저는 (스물일곱 살) 때까지 용돈을 받았어요.
I received an allowance until I was (27 years old).

Vocabulary Review

언제 when
부모님 parents
받다 to get, to receive
쓰다 to use, to spend
고등학교 high school
스물일곱 살 27 years old

-까지 until
용돈 pocket money, allowance
생활하다 to live (in a place)
대학교 college, university
스무 살 20 years old

언제까지 부모님께 용돈을 받아 생활했어요?

Seokjin's Answer

저는 직장을 얻기 전까지 용돈을 받았었어요. 대학교 4학년 때쯤 시작한 일이 있었는데 그 덕분에 부모님께 더 이상 손 벌리지 않고 돈을 모을 수 있었어요.

I received an allowance until I got a job. There was a job I started when I was in my 4th year of college, and thanks to that, I didn't have to rely on my parents for money anymore, and I could save my own money.

Study Notes

직장 job

전 before

용돈 pocket money

대학교 university, college

일 work, job

부모님 parents

손 벌리다 to get/borrow money from someone

돈 money

모으다 to collect, to gather, to save

-(으)ㄹ 수 있다 to be able to + V

얻다 to get, to gain, to obtain

-까지 until

받다 to get, to receive

시작하다 to start, to begin

덕분에 thanks to

더 이상 any more

A : 언제까지 부모님한테 용돈을 받았어요?

Until when did you receive an allowance from your parents?

B : 저는 지금도 부모님한테 용돈을 받아요.

Even now, I still receive an allowance from my parents.

A : 회사 다니는데 용돈을 받아요?

You have a job and you still receive an allowance?

B : 월급을 부모님이 관리하세요.

My parents manage my salary.

Vocabulary Review

언제까지 until when

부모님 parents

용돈 pocket money

받다 to get, to receive

지금도 even now

회사 company

다니다 to go (to a place regularly), to attend (regularly)

월급 salary, monthly pay

관리하다 to manage, to care for

주위 사람들한테 짠돌이라는 말 들어 본 적 있어요?

Have you ever heard people around you say you are a penny-pincher?

Similar Questions

주위 사람들한테 돈을 너무 안 쓴다는 말 들어 본 적 있어요?
Have you heard from people around you that you spend too little money?

주변 사람들한테 짠돌이라는 말 들어 본 적 있어요?
Have you ever heard people around you say you are a penny-pincher?

주변 사람들한테 돈을 너무 안 쓴다는 말 들어 본 적 있어요?
Have you ever heard people around you say that you hardly use your money?

Key Grammar Point

-한테

Person + -한테 = to/from + Person

Ex) 누구한테 들었어요? = **From whom did you hear that?**

네. 짠돌이라는 말 들어 본 적 있어요.

Yes. I've heard people say I'm a penny-pincher.

More Answers

네. 짠돌이라는 말 자주 들어요.

Yes. I often hear that I am a penny-pincher.

아니요. 짠돌이라는 말 들어 본 적 없어요.

No. I've never heard people say I am a cheapskate

아니요. 짠돌이라는 말 한 번도 안 들어 봤어요.

No. I've never heard people say I am a penny-pincher.

Vocabulary Review

주위 surrounding

짠돌이 cheapskate, penny-pincher

듣다 to listen

쓰다 to use, to spend

자주 often

한 번도 not even once

-(으)ㄴ 적(이) 있다 to have + V-ed (experience)

사람들 people

말 word, language, speech

너무 so, really, too much

주위 사람들한테 짠돌이라는 말 들어 본 적 있어요?

Jooyeon's Answer

아니요. 그런 말은 평생 한 번도 들어 본 적
이 없어요. 남들 앞에서 돈을 심하게 아끼거
나 안 쓰려고 하는 행동을 개인적으로도 별
로 좋아하지 않기 때문에 그런 말은 들어 보
지 못했어요.

No. I've never heard anyone say that about me in
my life. I personally don't like trying too hard to
save money or spending too little around other
people, so I haven't heard people say that about
me.

Study Notes

그런 such

평생 lifetime, one's whole life

남들 others

돈 money

아끼다 to save, to economize

-(으)려고 하다 to plan to + V

개인적으로 personally

별로 not really, not particularly

때문에 because

-(으)ㄴ 적(이) 없다 to not have + V-ed (experience)

말 word, language, speech

한 번도 not even once

앞 front

심하게 severely, terribly

쓰다 to use

행동 action, behavior

-도 also

좋아하다 to like

A : 지훈 씨, 주변 사람들한테 짠돌이라는 말 들어 본 적 있어요?

Ji-hoon, have you heard people around you say that you are a penny-pincher?

B : 네. 많죠.

Yes, a lot.

A : 그렇죠? 그럼 오늘은 지훈 씨가 쏘세요.

Right? Then, you pay this time, Ji-hoon.

B : 네? 제가 왜요? 다음에 살게요.

What? Why me? I will treat you next time.

Vocabulary Review

주변 surroundings, around

사람들 people

짠돌이 cheapskate, penny-pincher

말 word, language, speech

듣다 to listen

많다 to be a lot

그럼 then

오늘 today

왜 why

다음에 next

사다 to buy

(한 턱) 쏘다 to treat others, to pay for food for everybody

자신보다는 다른 사람을 위해 돈을 많이 쓰는 편이에요?

Do you tend to spend money on other people rather than yourself?

Similar Questions

자신을 위해서보다는 다른 사람을 위해서 돈을 많이 쓰는 편이에요?

Do you tend to spend money on other people rather than for yourself?

자기 자신한테보다 다른 사람한테 돈을 많이 쓰는 편이에요?

Do you tend to spend money on other people rather than on yourself?

자신보다는 다른 사람에게 쓰는 돈이 더 많은 편이에요?

Do you tend to spend more money on other people than yourself?

Key Grammar Point

-보다는

-보다 = more than / -는 = used for contrast

⇨ -보다는 = rather than, compared to

Ex) 이것보다는 저게 더 좋아요. = Rather than this, that one is better.

네. 저보다는 다른 사람을 위해 돈을 많이 쓰는 편이에요.

Yes. I tend to spend money on other people rather than myself.

More Answers

네. 저한테보다 다른 사람한테 돈을 많이 쓰는 편이에요.

Yes. I tend to spend more money on other people than on myself.

아니요. 저는 제 자신을 위해 돈을 많이 쓰는 편이에요.

No. I tend to spend a lot of money on myself.

아니요. 저는 제 자신한테 돈을 많이 쓰는 편이에요.

No. I tend to spend a lot of money on myself.

Vocabulary Review

자신 oneself

-보다 than

다른 different, other

사람 person

돈 money

쓰다 to use, to spend

-(으)ㄴ/는 편이다 to tend to, usually + V

자신보다는 다른 사람을 위해 돈을 많이 쓰는 편이에요?

Hyeonjeong's Answer

네, 그런 편인 거 같아요. 왠지 그로 인해서 기뻐하는 모습을 보는 게 좋아요. 그러려면 돈을 더 많이 벌어야겠네요.

Yes, I think I tend to be like that. Somehow, I like seeing people be happy because of that. For this reason, I guess I will have to make a lot of money.

Study Notes

-(으)ㄴ/는 편이다 to tend to; would usually + V

왠지 somehow, for some reason

그로 인해서 because of that, as a result of that

기뻐하다 to be glad, to be happy

모습 figure; looks, appearance

보다 to see, to watch

좋다 to be good, to like

돈 money

더 more

많이 a lot

(돈을) 벌다 to earn money, to make money

-아/어/여야겠다 should + V

A : 고은 씨는 자신보다는 다른 사람에게 쓰는 돈이 더 많은 편이에요?

Go-eun, do you tend to spend money on other people rather than yourself?

B : 아니요.

No.

A : 아, 그럼 자신을 위해 많이 써요?

Oh, then do you spend a lot on yourself?

B : 아니요. 저는 그냥 돈을 잘 안 써요. 그래서 별명이 짠돌이예요.

No. I just don't spend a lot of money. So my nickname is "cheapskate".

Vocabulary Review

자신 oneself

사람 person

돈 money

많다 to be a lot

별명 nickname

짠돌이 cheapskate, penny-pincher

다른 different, other

쓰다 to use, to spend

지출을 줄여야 하는 경우에 가장 먼저 소비를 줄일 수 있는 항목은 뭐예요?

What is the first item you could spend less on if you needed to cut down on spending?

Similar Questions

돈을 적게 써야 하는 경우에 가장 먼저 소비를 줄일 수 있는 항목은 뭐예요?
In the case of spending less money, what is the first item on which you could reduce on spending?

가장 먼저 소비를 줄일 수 있는 항목은 뭐예요?
What is the first item on which you can cut down on spending?

가장 먼저 지출을 줄일 수 있는 항목은 뭐예요?
What is the first item that you can spend less on?

Key Grammar Point

-(으)ㄴ/는 경우에

Verb stem + -(으)ㄴ/는 경우에 = in the case of + S + V-ing

Ex) 혼자 가는 경우에 = **if you go there alone, in the case of going there alone**

저는 (간식거리)에 쓰는 돈을 가장 먼저 줄일 수 있을 것 같아요.

I think I could reduce the money I spend on (snacks) first.

More Answers

저는 가장 먼저 (커피)에 쓰는 돈을 줄일 수 있을 것 같아요.
I think I could reduce the money I spend on (coffee) first.

저는 (외식)비를 가장 먼저 줄일 수 있을 것 같아요.
I think I could cut down the money I spend on (eating out) first.

저는 (교통)비를 가장 먼저 아낄 수 있을 것 같아요.
I think I could spend less on (transportation) fees first.

Vocabulary Review

지출 expense, spending

경우 case

먼저 first

항목 item

쓰다 to use, to spend

커피 coffee

-비 expense

-(으)ㄹ 수 있다 to be able to + V

-아/어/여야 하다 to have to + V, should + V

줄이다 to decrease, to lower, to reduce

가장 the most

소비 consumption

적다 to be few/little

간식거리 snacks

외식 eating out

교통 transportation

지출을 줄여야 하는 경우에 가장 먼저 소비를 줄일 수 있는 항목은 뭐예요?

Kyeong-eun's Answer

외식인 거 같아요. 외식하는 것도 좋아하고 주말에는 집에 있는 것보다는 외출을 자주 하는 편이라서 외식도 자주 하거든요.

I think it's eating out. I enjoy eating out too, and I often go out rather than staying at home on weekends, so I get to eat out often.

Study Notes

외식 eating out

좋아하다 to like

주말 weekend

집 house

-보다 than

외출 going out

자주 often

-(으)ㄴ/는 편이다 to tend to, usually + V

A : 저 올해는 꼭 생활비를 줄여 볼 거예요.
This year, I will absolutely try and reduce my living costs.

B : 좋은 생각이에요.
That's a good idea.

A : 가장 먼저 지출을 줄일 수 있는 항목이 뭘까요?
What would be something I could reduce spending on first?

B : 지금 저한테 물어보는 거예요? 음... 유진 씨는 옷이 너무 많은 것 같아요. 옷을 좀 적게 사 보세요.
Are you asking me now? Hmm... I think you, Yoojin, have too many clothes. Try buying fewer clothes.

Vocabulary Review

올해 this year

좋다 to be good, to like

가장 the most

지출 expense, spending

항목 item

옷 clothes

많다 to be a lot

적다 to be few/little

생활비 living expenses, the cost of living

줄이다 to decrease, to lower, to reduce

-아/어/여 보다 to try + -ing

꼭 to make sure + S + V, to be sure to + V

생각 thought

먼저 first

-(으)ㄹ 수 있다 to be able to + V

물어보다 to ask

너무 so, really, too much

좀 a little bit, kind of

사다 to buy

My Answers

Write your responses to the following questions below.

Q. 어떤 항목에 돈을 가장 많이 써요?

Q. 언제까지 부모님께 용돈을 받아 생활했어요?

Q. 주위 사람들한테 짠돌이라는 말 들어 본 적 있어요?

Q. 자신보다는 다른 사람을 위해 돈을 많이 쓰는 편이에요?

Q. 지출을 줄여야 하는 경우에 가장 먼저 소비를 줄일 수 있는 항목은 뭐예요?

10.
OBSESSION, ADDICTION, COMPULSIÓN

사람에게 집착해 본 적 있어요?

Have you ever been obsessed with anyone?

Similar Questions

누군가에게 집착해 본 적 있어요?

Have you ever been obsessed with someone?

어떤 사람에게 집착해 본 적 있어요?

Have you ever been obsessed with a person?

어떤 사람을 너무 좋아해서 집착해 본 적 있어요?

Have you ever liked someone so much that you were obsessed with him/her?

Key Grammar Point

너무 -아/어/여서

너무 + Verb stem + -아/어/여서 = Verb + so much that + ...

Ex) 너무 더워서 어지러워요. = **It's so hot that I'm dizzy.**

네. (남자 친구)한테 집착해 본 적 있어요.

Yes. I have been obsessed with a boyfriend once before.

More Answers

네. (어떤 여자)을/를 너무 좋아해서 집착해 본 적 있어요.

Yes. I have liked (a girl) so much and got obsessed with (her) before.

아니요. 사람한테 집착해 본 적 없어요.

No. I have never been obsessed with a person before.

아니요. 저는 사람한테 집착하는 타입이 아니에요.

No. I am not the type who becomes obsessed with a person.

Vocabulary Review

집착하다 to obsess

-(으)ㄴ 적(이) 있다 to have + V-ed (experience)

누군가 somebody

사람 person

너무 so, really, too much

좋아하다 to like

남자 친구 boyfriend

여자 female, girl

사람에게 집착해 본 적 있어요?

Kyung-hwa's Answer

저는 그 어떤 것에도 집착하지 않는 타입이라 '정이 없다', '차갑다'라는 말을 많이 들으면서 자랐는데, 그래도 사람은 한번 좋아하면 끝까지 좋아하는 타입인 것 같아요. 이게 집착인가요?

I am the type of person who doesn't get attached to anything easily, so I grew up hearing a lot of people say that I am "affectionless" and "cold", but I think that if I like someone, I like him/her forever. Is this obsession?

Study Notes

집착하다 to obsess

없다 to be not, to not have

말 word, language, speech

듣다 to listen

사람 person

좋아하다 to like

정 affection, attachment, love

차갑다 to be cold

많이 a lot

자라다 to grow

한번 once

끝까지 to the end

-(으)ㄴ 것 같다 to look like, to seem like, one thinks that + S + V

A : 연주 씨, 어떤 사람을 너무 좋아해서 집착해 본 적 있어요?

Yeon-joo, have you ever liked someone so much that you were obsessed with him?

B : 네. 사실 지금 집착하고 있는 거 같아요.

Yes. I think I am obsessed now.

A : 정말요? 그 사람이 누구예요?

Really? Who is that person?

B : 비밀이에요.

It's a secret.

Vocabulary Review

너무 so, really, too much

좋아하다 to like

집착하다 to obsess, to be obsessed

-(으)ㄴ 적(이) 있다 to have + V-ed (experience)

사실 fact, truth, actually

지금 now

-(으)ㄴ 것 같다 to look like, to seem like, one thinks that + S + V

비밀 secret

스스로를 완벽주의자라고 생각해요?

Do you think you are a perfectionist?

Similar Questions

스스로가 완벽주의자인 것 같아요?

Do you think you are a perfectionist?

스스로를 완벽주의자라고 느껴요?

Do you feel like you are a perfectionist?

자신이 완벽주의자라고 생각해요?

Do you think of yourself as a perfectionist?

Key Grammar Point

-(이)라고 느끼다

Noun + -(이)라고 느끼다 = to feel that + S + is + Noun

Ex) 실수라고 느껴요. = I feel that it's a mistake.

네. 저는 제가 완벽주의자라고 생각해요.

Yes. I think I am a perfectionist.

More Answers

네. 저는 제가 완벽주의자인 것 같아요.
Yes. I think I am a perfectionist.

아니요. 저는 완벽주의자가 아니라고 생각해요.
No. I think I am not a perfectionist.

아니요. 저는 스스로를 완벽주의자라고 생각하지 않아요.
No. I don't think I am a perfectionist.

Vocabulary Review

스스로 for oneself, oneself

완벽주의자 perfectionist

생각하다 to think

느끼다 to feel

자신 oneself

스스로를 완벽주의자라고 생각해요?

Seokjin's Answer

확실히 아닌 것 같아요. 제가 좋아하는 일을 할 때는 제 능력을 다 써서 좋은 결과물로 만들려고 하는 편이지만, 제가 별로 관심이 없거나 너무 어려운 일이라고 생각되면 '이 정도도 괜찮겠지.' 하며 더 진행하지 않는 경우가 많거든요.

I think I'm definitely not. When I do work that I like, I try to use all of my abilities to produce a good result, but when I am not so interested in something or find it too difficult, I often think "This should be good enough," and do not proceed further with it.

Study Notes

확실히 surely, certainly

일 work

쓰다 to use, to spend

만들다 to make

별로 not really, not particularly

없다 to be not, to not have

어렵다 to be difficult, to be hard

정도 level, degree, approximately

경우 case

좋아하다 to like

능력 ability, capacity

결과물 output

-(으)ㄴ/는 편이다 to tend to, usually + V

관심 interest

너무 so, really, too much

생각되다 to be considered, to be thought

괜찮다 to be okay, to be alright

진행하다 to carry out, to proceed with

A : 민준 씨는 자신이 완벽주의자라고 생각해요?

Min-joon, do you think you are a perfectionist?

B : 네. 저는 뭐든지 100% 마음에 들 때까지 다시 해야 직성이 풀려요.

Yes. I am not satisfied if I don't do something until I am 100% happy with the result.

A : 피곤할 것 같아요.

I think that must be tiring.

B : 아니에요. 마음에 들지 않는데 중간에 멈추는 게 더 스트레스예요.

No. It's more stressful to stop in the middle if I don't like it.

Vocabulary Review

자신 oneself

생각하다 to think

다시 again

피곤하다 to be tired

멈추다 to stop

더 more

마음에 들다 to be liked, to like, to find something likeable

완벽주의자 perfectionist

-까지 until

직성이 풀리다 to be satisfied

중간 middle, center

남에게 지는 걸 싫어하는 성격이에요?

Are you the type of person who hates losing to someone?

Similar Questions

지는 걸 싫어하는 성격이에요?

Are you the type of person that hates losing?

무엇에든 지는 걸 싫어하는 성격이에요?

Are you the type of person who hates losing in anything?

남에게 지기 싫어하는 성격이에요?

Are you the type of person who hates losing to someone?

Key Grammar Point

-는 성격이다

Verb stem + -는 성격이다 = to be the type of person that + Verb

Ex) 저는 걱정을 많이 하는 성격이에요.

= I am the type of person that worries a lot.

네. 저는 남에게 지는 걸 싫어하는 성격이에요.

Yes. I am the type of person who hates losing.

More Answers

네. 저는 남에게 지는 걸 굉장히 싫어해요.
Yes. I really hate losing.

아니요. 저는 승부에 연연하지 않는 편이에요.
No. I usually do not cling to whether I win or lose.

아니요. 저는 이기고 지는 것에 연연하지 않는 편이에요.
No. I'm usually not attached to whether I win or lose.

Vocabulary Review

남 others
싫어하다 to hate
무엇에든 anything, whatever
승부 winning and losing
연연하다 to cling to, to stick to
이기다 to win

지다 to lose
성격 character, personality
굉장히 very, extremely

남에게 지는 걸 싫어하는 성격이에요?

Jooyeon's Answer

누구든 그렇겠지만 저도 지는 것보단 이기는 게 좋아요. 하지만 이기는 것에 목숨을 걸거나 지는 것을 심하게 억울해한다거나 하진 않아요. 중요한 일이라면 이기려고 최선을 다하겠지만 그렇지 않다면 별로 신경 쓰지 않는 편이에요.

I think it's the same with everybody, but I like winning rather than losing. However, I don't put myself on the line over winning or be terribly sulky about losing. If it's an important thing, I would try my best to win, but if not, I tend to not care so much.

Study Notes

누구든지 anybody

지다 to lose

이기다 to win

목숨을 걸다 to risk one's life to

중요하다 to be important

-(으)려고 in order to

별로 not really, not particularly

-(으)ㄴ/는 편이다 to tend to; usually + V

그렇다 to be so

-보다 than

좋다 to be good, to like

심하게 severely, terribly

일 work, job

최선을 다하다 to do one's best

신경 쓰다 to care about, to worry about

억울해하다 to be bitter, to feel that something unfair has been done to oneself

A : 우리 아이가 잘 적응할 수 있을지 걱정이에요.

I am worried whether (or not) our child will be able to adjust well.

B : 잘 적응할 거예요. 걱정하지 마세요.

He will adapt well. Don't worry.

A : 남에게 지는 걸 정말 싫어하는 성격이라서요.

He really doesn't like losing to other people.

B : 그게 장점이 될 수도 있어요.

That can be an advantage.

Vocabulary Review

아이 kid, child

남 others

싫어하다 to hate

성격 character, personality

장점 strong point, advantage

되다 to become

-(으)ㄹ 수도 있다 may + V

적응하다 to adapt, to get used to, to adjust

걱정이다 to be worried

지다 to lose

한 가지 일에 얼마나 오래 집중할 수 있어요?

How long can you focus on one thing?

Similar Questions

한 가지 일에 얼마나 오랫동안 집중할 수 있어요?

How long can you focus on one thing?

얼마나 오랫동안 한 가지 일에 집중할 수 있어요?

How long are you able to focus on one thing?

한 번에 얼마나 오래 집중할 수 있어요?

How long can you focus at once?

Key Grammar Point

얼마나

얼마나 + 오래/오랫동안 = for how long

Ex) 얼마나 오래 기다렸어요? = **For how long did you wait?**

저는 (세) 시간 정도는 집중할 수 있어요.

I can focus for about (three) hours.

More Answers

저는 (두세) 시간 정도는 안 쉬고 집중할 수 있어요.
I can focus on something without stopping for about (two to three) hour(s).

저는 (다섯) 시간 정도는 집중할 수 있을 것 같아요.
I think I can focus on something for about (five) hour(s).

저는 (한) 시간도 채 집중 못 할 것 같아요.
I don't think I can focus for even (one) hour(s).

Vocabulary Review

일 work, job

오래 long, for a long time

-(으)ㄹ 수 있다 to be able to + V

시간 time

쉬다 to rest

한 가지 one thing, one kind (of), one sort (of)

채 ~ 못하다 can't even do (as much as) ...

얼마나 how (much)

집중하다 to concentrate

적어도 at least

정도 level, degree, approximately

한 가지 일에 얼마나 오래 집중할 수 있어요?

Hyeonjeong's Answer

어떤 일이냐에 따라 다른 거 같아요. 제가 좋아하는 일이라면 15시간도 가능해요. 그래도 나이를 먹으니 중간중간 좀 쉬어 줘야 하지만요.

I think it depends on what kind of stuff it is. If it's something I like, even 15 hours is possible. Since I've gotten older, though, I do have to take breaks from time to time.

Study Notes

어떤 which
일 work, job
-에 따라 다르다 to depend on; to vary depending on
좋아하다 to like
가능하다 to be possible
나이를 먹다 to grow old
중간중간 midway, halfway
쉬다 to rest

A : 광수 씨는 한 번에 얼마나 오래 집중할 수 있어요?

Gwang-soo, how long can you focus on something at once?

B : 12시간 동안 밥 먹는 것도 잊어버리고 일한 적 있어요.

I have worked for 12 hours straight before and even forgot to eat.

A : 진짜요? 배 안 고팠어요?

Really? Weren't you hungry?

B : 집중했더니 배고픈지도 몰랐어요.

I was focused and I didn't even know I was hungry.

Vocabulary Review

한 번 once

오래 long, for a long time

밥 먹다 to eat (a meal)

잊어버리다 to forget

일하다 to work

배고프다 to be hungry

모르다 to not know

-(으)ㄴ 적(이) 있다 to have + V-ed (experience)

얼마나 how (much)

집중하다 to concentrate

스스로의 힘으로 중독에서 벗어나 본 적 있어요?

Have you ever overcome an addiction on your own?

Similar Questions

스스로의 힘으로 중독에서 빠져나와 본 적 있어요?

Have you ever overcome an addiction on your own?

남의 도움 없이 중독에서 빠져나와 본 적 있어요?

Have you ever gotten out of an addiction without anybody's help?

스스로의 힘으로 중독을 이겨 내 본 적 있어요?

Have you ever beat an addiction on your own?

Key Grammar Point

없이

Noun + 없이 = without + 없이

Ex) 인터넷 없이 살 수 없어요. = **I can't live without the Internet.**

네. 저는 스스로의 힘으로 (콜라) 중독에서 벗어나 본 적 있어요.

Yes. I have had the experience of overcoming an addiction to (Coca-Cola) on my own.

More Answers

네. 저는 스스로의 힘으로 (니코틴) 중독에서 벗어나는 데 성공한 적 있어요.

Yes. I have succeeded in overcoming (nicotine) addiction on my own before.

아니요. 저는 아직도 (카페인) 중독에서 벗어나지 못했어요.

No. I still haven't overcome my (caffeine) addiction.

아니요. 저는 아직도 (게임) 중독에서 빠져나오지 못했어요.

No. I still haven't overcome my (gaming) addiction.

Vocabulary Review

스스로 for oneself, oneself

도움 help

이겨 내다 to overcome

카페인 caffeine

아직도 still, yet

벗어나다 to break the habit of, to get away from

-(으)ㄴ 적(이) 있다 to have + V-ed (experience)

빠져나오다 to get out of, to escape

남 others, someone you are not related to

힘 power

없이 without

콜라 Coca-Cola

성공하다 to succeed

중독 addiction, poisoning

스스로의 힘으로 중독에서 벗어나 본 적 있어요?

Kyeong-eun's Answer

커피를 좋아하는데 그게 중독일 수도 있을 거 같아서 '한 달 동안 커피 안 마시기'를 해 본 적이 있어요. 딱 한 달 동안 커피를 안 마셨고 그러고 나서 다시 마시기 시작했어요.

I like coffee, and I thought it might be an addiction so I have tried "not-drinking-coffee-for-a-month" before. I didn't drink coffee for exactly one month and after that, I started drinking it again.

Study Notes

커피 coffee

중독 addiction; poisoning

한 달 one month

동안 during

마시다 to drink

-(으)ㄴ 적(이) 있다 to have + V-ed (experience)

딱 just, exactly

다시 again

시작하다 to start, to begin

좋아하다 to like

-(으)ㄹ 수도 있다 may + V

A : 담배 끊으세요. 몸에 안 좋아요.

Quit smoking. It's bad for your body.

B : 저 마음만 먹으면 언제든지 끊을 수 있어요. 저 스스로의 힘으로 게임 중독에서 벗어나 본 적도 있어요.

If I make up my mind, I can always quit. I have gotten out of a gaming addiction on my own before.

A : 그럼 지금 당장 끊으면 되겠네요.

Then, you can just quit right now.

B : 아니에요. 내년 1월부터 끊을 생각이에요.

No. I am planning to quit next January.

Vocabulary Review

담배 cigarette

언제든지 whenever

스스로 for oneself, oneself

중독 addiction, poisoning

지금 now

내년 next year

몸에 안 좋다 to be not good for health

마음 먹다 to decide, to make one's mind

벗어나다 to break the habit of, to get away from

-(으)ㄴ 적(이) 있다 to have + V-ed (experience)

끊다 to quit (smoking or other habits)

-(으)ㄹ 수 있다 to be able to + V

힘 power

그럼 then

당장 right now, immediately

생각 thought

My Answers

Write your responses to the following questions below.

Q. 사람에게 집착해 본 적 있어요?

Q. 스스로를 완벽주의자라고 생각해요?

Q. 남에게 지는 걸 싫어하는 성격이에요?

Q. 한 가지 일에 얼마나 오래 집중할 수 있어요?

Q. 스스로의 힘으로 중독에서 벗어나 본 적 있어요?

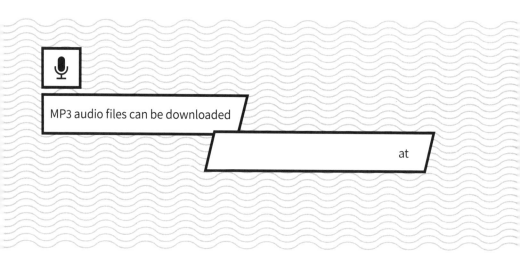

MP3 audio files can be downloaded

at

http://TalkToMeInKorean.com/audio

Head on over to the online store,
MyKoreanStore.com,
to check out more E-Books
which are not available in paperback
as well as digital E-Book versions
of certain paperback books.